WAYS OF TELLING

WAYS OF TELLING

Examining Stories at Key Stage 4

MIKE ROYSTON

Stanley Thornes (Publishers) Ltd

This edition first published in 1996 by:
Stanley Thornes (Publishers) Ltd
Ellenborough House
Wellington Street
CHELTENHAM GL50 1YW
England

96 97 98 99 00 / 10 9 8 7 6 5 4 3 2 1

A catalogue record for this book is available from the British Library.

ISBN 0–7487–2237–8

Cover artwork by Raynor Design
Illustrated by Dick Barton
Printed and bound in Great Britain at
T J Press (Padstow) Ltd, Cornwall

Acknowledgements

The author would like to thank Bess Clarke, Finham Park School, Coventry, and GCSE students at The Billericay School, Essex, for their help in trialling material for this book.

The author and publishers are grateful to the following for permission to use copyright material:

Christine Green on behalf of the author for Maeve Binchy, 'Telling Stories' • HarperCollins Publishers for Leslie Halward, 'The Breadwinner' in *Shorties*, ed. Roy Blatchford, Unwin Hyman, 1987 • Penguin Books Ltd for Stan Barstow, 'One Wednesday Afternoon' from *The Desperadoes and Other Stories* by Stan Barstow, Michael Joseph, 1961. Copyright © 1961 Stan Barstow; and Robert Westall, 'Woman and Home' from *The Call and Other Stories* by Robert Westall, Viking Children's Books, 1989. Copyright © 1989 Robert Westall • Laurence Pollinger on behalf of the author for Ella Griffiths, 'The Dead Don't Steal' • Random Century UK Ltd for Bernard MacLaverty, 'Father and Son', Jonathan Cape, 1982, 1987 • Mari Beinset Waagaard for 'The Sweet Old Lady Who Cried Wolf' • Kate Walker for 'Love Letters' first published in *State of the Heart*, ed. P E Matthews, Omnibus Books Australia, 1988.

Also the following for permission to reproduce copyright photographs:

Format/Joanne O'Brien (posed by models), p.9 • Carl and Melanie Gray © Simon Diffey, p.94 • Simon Marsden, p.67 • Network/Gideon Mendel, p.116 • Photofusion/Gina Glover, p.47 • Photofusion/Anna Jauncey, p.31.

Every effort has been made to trace all the copyright holders, but if any have been inadvertently overlooked the publishers will be pleased to make the necessary arrangement at the first opportunity.

Contents

To the teacher

INTENTIONS

Ways of Telling is a teaching anthology of paired stories for GCSE/Standard Grade courses. Its six Units are designed to:

- introduce students to a comprehensive range of story-telling forms and styles.
- focus attention on the key elements of narrative fiction – plot and structure, character presentation, use of dialogue, style and language, setting and atmosphere, varieties of viewpoint.
- provide self-contained schemes of work which incorporate speaking and listening activities, a repertoire of writing tasks, and exercises in literary response.
- instruct students in comparing the style and subject-matter of shorter fictions, to support the comparative study of literature now prescribed for all GCSE examinations.
- complement the teaching of novels, the chief elements of which are mirrored in miniature in the short-story form.

STORY SELECTION

Most of the stories have been written recently and are not normally found in GCSE anthologies. They have been chosen because:

- classroom trialling indicates that students aged 14–17 find their topicality appealing and relevant to their own concerns.
- they are stories of high quality in their own right and, when paired, illuminate each other in interesting and instructive ways.
- they are accessible to Key Stage 4 students across the ability range.
- collectively, they cover a broad spectrum of fictional genres.
- they derive from a variety of cultural traditions – English, Scottish, Welsh, Northern and Southern Irish, American, Australian and Scandinavian.

Unit design

Each Unit is built around two stories comparable in theme and/or form and style. The Units contain:

- preliminary activities for small groups and pairs, to establish an appropriate context for students before they read each story.
- a post-reading 'speaking and listening' activity (role-play, 'hot seating', improvisation, etc.) to increase students' personal involvement with the text.
- 'understanding' and 'response' sections designed to deepen students' perception of what they have read and to highlight, through discussion and writing, specific story-telling devices.
- a varied choice of writing tasks: creative, re-creative, empathetic, discursive and analytical.
- an End-of-Unit section requiring students to evaluate the paired stories' themes and narrative techniques.

Activities within each Unit, and throughout the book as a whole, have been planned to develop students' reading and response skills in a progressive way.

Outcomes

The book's activities are geared to current GCSE examination requirements. They fulfil the National Curriculum criteria on which these are based by:

- generating evidence of achievement in speaking and listening, for which the paired stories provide a stimulating context and a clear focus.
- providing opportunities for the widest possible range of writing.
- assisting students to read stories by responding to the ways in which they are written, rather than by using an indiscriminate 'comprehension' approach.
- equipping students with the skills which allow them to conduct an informed analysis of writers' methods – skills which need to be systematically taught if students are to meet the difficult challenge of GCSE examinations in their new form.

To the student

This book is made up of twelve short stories. They can be used for GCSE coursework and to prepare for English or English Literature examinations.

Most of the stories have been written recently and are about life in the present day. About half of them look at various aspects of teenagers' experience. The rest examine a range of wider issues, as the Unit titles show.

The book is divided into six Units, each containing two stories linked together in a certain way. Sometimes the link has to do with what the stories are about; for example, 'Heartaches' and 'Families'. Sometimes it is because of the *kind* of stories they are; for example, 'Crimes' and 'Mysteries'.

There is a mixture of Speaking and Writing activities on each story. These require you to work in a variety of ways – in small groups, in pairs, by yourself, and as a whole class. The order of activities means that you will never be asked to write about the stories without first exploring them through other means, such as role-play, group discussion, improvisation, class debate, and so on.

The title of the book, *Ways of Telling,* indicates how it will be useful to your English studies. For GCSE, you need to show your understanding of *how* writers tell their stories, as well as explaining what they are about. This book, therefore, contains stories written in many different styles.

As you work on the stories, you should gain confidence in your own 'ways of telling' why they were written as they were and whether the writers succeed in what they set out to do.

UNIT ONE

CRIMES

The Sweet Old Lady Who Cried Wolf

Mari Waagaard

In *The Sweet Old Lady Who Cried Wolf*, two women plan to murder each other for quite different reasons. Will either, or both, succeed?

The Dead Don't Steal

Ella Griffiths

The Dead Don't Steal is also a murder story. How does a murdered woman manage to turn herself into a car thief when her corpse is lying exactly where the killer left it?

1 Pre-reading activity on both stories

Speaking and listening *Get out of that!*

a **In a group**, read the following crime scenario.

Walking home by yourself from school, you pass a large detached house. It is the home of an elderly couple known to your family. The couple are away on holiday. Their burglar alarm is ringing.

You decide to investigate. Still carrying your school bag, you make your way to the back of the house. No one sees you. The glass panel in the kitchen door has been broken, and the door is half-open. You step inside.

In the lounge, the scene is one of total chaos. Furniture has been overturned, drawers and their contents are scattered across the floor, and a display cabinet containing expensive china ornaments has obviously been ransacked. Quite a few items from the display cabinet are still lying on the carpet; the rest have apparently been stolen. There is no sign of the burglar(s).

Shocked and tense, you are still thinking clearly enough to pick up the phone and dial 999. As you are giving information about the break-in and burglary, you hear the siren of a police car approaching outside. At the moment you finish your 999 call, two uniformed officers enter the house.

You suddenly realise that *you* are under suspicion.

This is the evidence against you:

- The time is 2.50 pm. You should still be in school. The police are dubious about your story that you felt unwell after a games lesson and left school without telling the office.
- It rained during the morning. The only footprints the police can find in the kitchen match your shoes exactly.
- Because your family is friendly with the couple, it is established that you have visited the house before. You know, of course, about the china ornaments in the display cabinet.
- You do an evening paper-round in the district. You are therefore aware that the couple are away for a fortnight's holiday.
- Your fingerprints are everywhere. You also, without realising it, slightly cut your hand as you pushed open the glass-panelled kitchen door.

- The police are not impressed when you say you dialled 999 to tell them about the burglary. Apparently it is quite common for burglars to do this in a disguised voice before they leave the scene of a break-in.

- Your large school bag is standing on the lounge carpet surrounded by china ornaments. Apart from your games kit and a few books, your bag is empty.

- When the police later examine your confidential file at school, they see that you were caught last year stealing money from a coat pocket in the cloakroom.

b **As a group**, look at all the details in the scenario and make a list, with the benefit of hindsight, of the things you did wrong.

c Discuss how you can prove your innocence to the police, bearing in mind the evidence against you.

d Once you have decided how to prove your innocence, finish this activity by *either* holding a **class discussion** in which everyone pools their ideas, *or* by remaining **in your group** and role-playing the formal interview you have at the police station where you are taken for questioning. Two members of the group play the parts of CID officers and other group members take on between them the role of the 'suspect'.

Now read *The Sweet Old Lady Who Cried Wolf*

THE SWEET OLD LADY WHO CRIED WOLF

One day the sweet old lady came into the police station and said, 'Forgive my disturbing you again, Inspector, but you see, there's a dead body in my garden.'

She leaned confidentially across the desk and whispered, 'He's such a nice elderly gentleman. He's lying in my poppy bed in such a peculiar, twisted attitude. And there's a knife in his back too. I'm certain this must be foul play, Inspector; wilful and cold blooded murder, don't you think?'

Chief Constable Ole Gregersen looked at Thea Dahl, his new assistant, and made a sign to her. Then he bent down and patted the sweet old lady on the arm and said reassuringly, 'Come now Mrs Werle. Are you quite sure you saw a body? You may be mistaken, you know. Have another look. And promise me,' he pointed a mock-threatening finger, 'promise me you'll stop reading all that nonsense you're filling your pretty little head with. All those detective stories aren't good for you, you're much too sensitive and imaginative. Promise, Mrs Werle! Now, you be a good girl…'

The sweet old lady blushed, looked reproachfully at the policeman and muttered under her breath as she turned to leave the station, 'My, oh my, Inspector, you're incorrigible – and a great tease too. But I'll do as I'm told. I'll walk straight home and have another look. But I'm sure the gentleman with the knife will still be there. It's a shame. Anyway…Good day to you, Inspector, and to you too, Miss.'

Thea Dahl gazed appalled at her superior. 'For heaven's sake, Mr Gregersen, what if the woman's telling the truth? There *might* be a dead man in her garden. You really shouldn't snub her like that, Sir, a sweet old lady like her!'

Mr Gregersen grinned then sighed and said musingly,

'You're new here. If you weren't, you'd know that this little old lady, Agnete Werle, pops in every month or so to report crimes. Crimes which only exist in her imagination, that is. A murder, a theft, a swindle. You remember when Edward Munch's "Vampire" was stolen from the Munch Museum? She turned up regularly once a week and told us where we could find the painting. It was even hanging in her sitting-room! As we didn't know her then we sent a couple of the boys to check, just in case, but of course it was sheer nonsense. Actually we checked false reports of thefts and murders on several occasions and gave her quite a talking-to. She just looked at us with those innocent blue eyes and said she was sorry! She is very sweet but more than a bit eccentric and I think a little bit soft in the head too. But don't worry, I won't offend her or hurt her. After all, she wouldn't hurt a fly.'

Gregersen paused and thought for a while, then went on, 'I feel sorry for her, in a way, although she seems happy enough. She's rich, mind you – rolling in money and she lives in a beautiful house, all inherited from her husband. He was a war hero – fought in the resistance against the Nazis.'

Thea Dahl listened attentively. 'Does she really live by herself? She must be quite an age.'

'As a matter of fact she's in her eighties but she's fit as a fiddle. Alone, yes, but there's a woman who comes in to clean the house once a week and I think she rents out a room to a female student just to have a young person around, not for the cash of course; and she certainly is generous with her money…'

Meanwhile the young tenant in Mrs Werle's house, Ellida Wang, was deep in conversation with her boyfriend, Jorgen. Both 'students', both unemployed, both very broke, both obsessed with the idea of getting hold of money, lots of money, in the easiest way possible. They had tried burglary and the like without success and had so far avoided the police.

But now there was a chance of realising their dreams. Money, exciting journeys, *la dolce vita*…Let us listen for a moment to their interesting conversation.

Jorgen: To hell with your crappy sentimentality. It's settled now. The old bat has absolutely no use for all that cash. Damn Amnesty or Save the Children or whatever she gives it to. It's you and me who need to be saved – before we die of boredom and poverty.

Ellida: Okay, okay. But I can't help feeling a bit sorry for the old girl. I mean, she is very sweet in a way. And she relies on me. She's even told me she'll give me some money when I've graduated.

Jorgen: Shut up, idiot! When did you manage to pass an exam in your life? No, we've got to do the job. Remember, she's worth two million. It'll be like taking a lollipop from a baby.

Ellida: She's cleverer than you think, hides her dough pretty cunningly…Hey, look out of the window! Here she comes, toddling along. Look at her smile and that white hair – and look at that crazy hat!

Jorgen: Don't go all soft on her now. You weren't all that soft when we did over that old couple, remember? You laughed your head off when that old bloke saw his pension disappear…Well, I'd better make myself scarce before the old lady catches me.

Ellida was sitting with Ibsen's 'The Doll House' propped in front of her when Mrs Werle entered, flushed and breathless after her quick walk.

She beamed when she saw Ellida studying so diligently in the huge library.

'That's right, my dear. I see you're working hard and using my library as I told you to do. You'll find all the books you'll need here, classics and the moderns. But isn't it time you were off, Ellida? It's Wednesday: there's that lecture in old Norwegian literature this afternoon, the one you told me about, remember?'

When the young woman was out of sight Mrs Werle went straight to one of the shelves. She pulled out a couple of books. Between Doyle's "A Study in

Scarlet" and Chesterton's "The Innocence of Father Brown" was a small tape recorder neatly hidden away.

It *had* to succeed this time.

Agnete Werle sat down in her best chair, rewound the tape and listened. She heard it all. 'To hell with your crappy sentimentality...we've got to do the job...worth two million...like taking a lollipop from a baby.'

Mrs Werle listened very carefully. She didn't miss a word. Then she played the whole conversation from the beginning again.

Oh yes, oh yes, she said and nodded repeatedly.

The she took out a book by one of her favourite writers, Patricia Highsmith. But she had not read more than a few pages of *The Talented Mr Ripley* when she lowered the book and began to hum softly.

She always did, when she was planning something.

'Hi, Mrs Werle! I've come straight from the lecture and I hope you don't mind my friend, he's a student too. Jorgen, meet Mrs Werle. Mrs Werle, this is Jorgen Thomassen, my – er – fiancé.'

Agnete started. She must have dozed off in her best chair with the book lying in her lap. Fortunately she had hidden the little tape recorder. She looked at her visitors; slim bodies dressed in almost similar sweaters, jeans and sneakers. Two quite good-looking youngsters if it hadn't been for that watchful greedy look on their faces – oh yes – even on Ellida's, that was quite obvious now.

She said slowly, 'Any friend of Ellida's is a friend of mine. Glad to meet you, young man. You go to medical school, is that so? You'll end up as a surgeon, then – and Ellida studies art and she'll be a teacher in grammar school. Oh, you'll be successful, the two of you! Have you got far in your studies, Mr Thomassen?'

'Just a year or two left. But call me Jorgen, please. Ellida's your good friend and—'

'We have grown quite close, that's right. But do sit down, I'll make you a meal. You young people must be hungry.'

The old lady went off towards the kitchen, beaming and talking. 'I'll make you a really nice snack. Tea and sandwiches – relax, both of you! – make yourself at home, Jorgen, the way Ellida does. Oh, it's so lovely to have young people in the house.'

There was a pause. The boy and girl looked at each other. Jorgen tapped one finger against his head in a meaningful way.

'My young friends, I have a splendid idea!' Agnete almost ran into the sitting room again, clapping her hands in joy. 'Now listen. Ellida, I'm sure you remember that I've shown you all the rooms in the house *except* one. The secret room – the exciting room, Ellida!'

'Do you mean the bomb-proof room your husband built just before the second world war, is that the one?'

'Exactly, my dear,' cried Agnete, as if inspired. 'My husband had a very important and trusted position in the resistance movement during the German occupation. He was helping people escape to Sweden and Britain. That special room was so well hidden it was a marvellous place for anyone who had to hide from the Nazis, and for other people too…It's under the cellar, beautifully furnished with a thick carpet on the floor and book shelves and expensive paintings – it's the most exciting, most bomb-proof and best secret room in Oslo, maybe in the whole of Norway! To show you how much I appreciate having you here I want us to celebrate in what is, for me, the most sacred room in the whole world. But now, I must finish in the kitchen. It won't take a minute.'

She disappeared again. Jorgen grinned at Ellida. He was holding a heavy silver candlestick in his hand, examining it.

Agnete reappeared out of breath, her cheeks rosy.

'Oh, I'm so looking forward to celebrating in there with you. Jorgen, you take this – oh, please don't fiddle with that candlestick, my cleaner isn't too fond of polishing silver and neither am I. By the way, there are two marvellous candelabra in the secret room, pure gold, you'll see. If you want something stronger than tea there's plenty to drink down there…Here we go. I'll lead the way.' Agnete smiled at them. She was all joy and enthusiasm.

'Watch it now, Ellida, here comes our chance,' whispered Jorgen as they followed the old lady down the cellar stairs and beyond, along the corridor lit by a faint bulb in the ceiling.

Eventually Agnete stopped in front of a massive half-open door. She turned to the young couple, extending her arms invitingly.

'Here we are. Please go in – and put the tea things on the little table over there in the corner. We'll have a grand time, the three of us! There's plenty of wine and sherry in the corner cupboard. Now, in you go.'

'Oh, Mrs Werle, it's awfully dark in here. Can you put on the light ? We can't see a thing.'

'Just a second, dear. There's a switch here in the corridor, here it is. Oh, my, the door's shutting! And it's so heavy, impossible to open from this side...! Well, well, well – it can't be helped. You'll have to celebrate alone in there, my dears. Take your time.'

And Agnete Werle bolted the heavy door with great care.

Standing for a moment outside, listening, she could scarcely hear their shouts. Faint, oh so faint were the voices heard here in the corridor. And nothing at all could be heard from anywhere else in the house. Nothing at all. This she knew for certain. Not even the screaming and shouting of that traitor, the Norwegian Nazi, himself a torturer, had been heard in that autumn of 1943. Served him right, the rough treatment he'd got.

No room in the world could be more soundproof. And no room could be more hermetically sealed – when the valves in the ventilator were closed. They were now. They could be regulated from the corridor.

'I hope they drink their tea first. It will put them to sleep quite gently,' murmured the old lady on her way upstairs. Ever so gently she chuckled as she sat down in her favourite chair with *The Talented Mr Ripley*.

She looked forward to reading it, then to watching a 'Poirot' film on the telly at ten o'clock sharp.

'*Carpe diem*, that's a good maxim,' said Agnete Werle, pleased.

'Excuse me, Inspector, I've got something very important to tell you today.'

Chief Constable Ole Gregersen looked at the old lady with a resigned expression. There was a troubled look in her bright blue eyes. Her hat was askew on her snow-white hair and her small thin fingers were clasping her handbag. No way could he be angry with her, she was such a sweet pathetic creature.

'What extraordinary things have happened now, Mrs Werle?' he asked patiently, far more patiently than he felt.

'I think something really peculiar and sinister has happened in my house, Mr Gregersen. There are actually *two* bodies, in my cellar. A young man and woman.'

'With knives in their backs, I presume?'

He winked mischievously and made a face at his assistant, Thea Dahl.

'No, no, Inspector, nothing of the sort! Would you imagine it, they're strangled, *choked*, both of them. Anyway, their faces are quite blue. Isn't it terrible? Do you think the murderer will be caught, Mr Gregersen?'

The policeman gave a sigh.

'You just go home to that nice house of yours and have another look and you'll find that everything's all right...But mind you, no more mystery books from now on. Why don't you read something nice, something edifying and uplifting for a change? Well, goodbye to you.'

The old lady walked slowly to the door, then abruptly turned round with a stern look at the policeman, cocking her head.

'What if I told you, Inspector, that I was the culprit – that it was I who killed the two poor creatures? Then you'd have to arrest me, wouldn't you, Mr Gregersen?'

'Shame on you, Mrs Werle! You are a wicked old lady, aren't you, in spite of being so sweet.' He took her gently by the arm and escorted her to the door.

'And now, Mrs Werle, please don't bother us again with that vivid imagination of yours.'

'All right, Inspector, I'll do as I'm told. But listen, shall I let the couple stay in the locked room in the cellar and never go into the room again as long as I live?'

'That's right, madam. Now off you go, have a nice walk home, and remember if someone is ever really unkind to you or tries to be violent – you know how young people can behave these days – you come straight here to us. It's lucky you don't live very far away.'

'Very well, Inspector. I'm glad to know there is some goodness in this cruel world. Goodbye, Mr Gregersen, and good day to you, Miss. And *thank you* with all my heart.'

The sweet old lady gave them a friendly nod and tripped out of the office.

Thea Dahl looked inquiringly at her superior.

'What on earth did she thank us like that for?'

'Hard to tell. She's very polite and well-bred, so why not? Well, she *is*, in spite of her crazy ideas.'

'Eccentric but harmless, isn't that how you put it, sir?'

'That right, Miss Dahl. Eccentric but harmless.' The Chief Constable nodded, pleased with this apt description.

MARI WAAGAARD

2 Post-reading activity on *The Sweet Old Lady Who Cried Wolf*

Speaking and listening *Causes and consequences*

a **In a group**, decide on the best statement you can to fill each blank in the five 'cause and consequence' items below. Refer back to the story as you do so. Make a note of what you decide.

1 At the start of the story, the **cause** of Mrs Werle going to the police station is ________________________________.

The **consequence** is ________________________________.

2 The **cause** of the conversation between Ellida and Jorgen on page 13 is ________________________________.

The **consequence** is ________________________________.

3 The **cause** of Mrs Werle listening to the tape recording of Ellida and Jorgen's conversation is ________________________________.

The **consequence** is ________________________________.

4 The **cause** of Mrs Werle suggesting that Ellida and Jorgen should visit her husband's special room is ________________________________.

The **consequence** is ________________________________.

5 The **cause** of Mrs Werle re-visiting the police station at the end of the story is ________________________________.

The **consequence** is ________________________________.

b Finish this activity by holding a **class discussion** in which you compare your cause and consequence statements with those of other groups.

3 Text focus

Reading for understanding

a **In a group**, search the story for evidence that Mrs Werle leads a 'double life'. Discuss in particular:

- the impression of herself she gives to the police.
- the impression of herself she gives to Ellida and Jorgen.
- her fondness for crime stories, especially murders.
- her liking for deception and intrigue.

b **With a partner**, look closely at the way the writer presents Ellida and Jorgen to us. Say, with reasons, whether you think:

- we are meant to feel sorry for what happens to them.
- we are meant to feel they get what they deserve.
- we are meant to have mixed feelings about their deaths.

c **As a class**, discuss Mrs Werle's motives for murdering the two students.

The writer leaves you to make up your own mind about this. As long as you can find evidence from the story, put forward your own theory or theories.

d **By yourself**, write on the following topic:

'Although clever, Agnete Werle is a twisted character who, as the story shows, has sinister motives for murder. She ought to be locked away for life.'

How far do you agree?

Reading and response

e **As a class**, or **in groups**, consider two aspects of Mari Waagaard's story-telling technique by discussing the questions which follow:

Suspense

(i) What do you understand by the term 'suspense'? Give examples from films and from other stories and novels you have read.

(ii) *The Sweet Old Lady Who Cried Wolf* is meant to keep the reader guessing. Does it succeed? In discussing this, try to recall your reactions when you first read the story, and say:

- what you thought of Mrs Werle at the very start.
- what you thought would happen after reading the students' conversation on page 13.
- what you thought Mrs Werle's reasons were for using the hidden tape recorder.
- what you thought was likely to happen when Mrs Werle took Ellida and Jorgen to the 'secret room'.
- what you thought would happen when Mrs Werle returned to the police station at the end.

(iii) Overall, do you feel the writer manages to create enough suspense to hold your interest throughout the story? Give reasons to back up your opinion.

Viewpoint

(i) What is meant by the term 'viewpoint'? Think of any novel or films you know where the story is told from more than one the point of view.

(ii) In *The Sweet Old Lady Who Cried Wolf*, the viewpoint keeps changing. Where do we see Mrs Werle from the point of view of:

- Chief Constable Ole Gregerson?
- Ellida and Jorgen?
- the writer herself?

(iii) What effects does Mari Waagaard gain by portraying Mrs Werle from several viewpoints? Do you think they add to, or detract from, the success of the story? Say why.

f **By yourself**, write a brief account of Mari Waagaard's use of suspense. Say whether you think it adds to the story's interest – and, if so, how.

Now read *The Dead Don't Steal*

THE DEAD DON'T STEAL

The ringing of the phone on his desk brought Curt Lessner's head up with a jerk. Every time it rang he was afraid it was the police.

This time it was – the Traffic Division.

'Morning, Mr Lessner,' a friendly Bergen voice said. 'Inspector Svendsen here. We've found your car. At least, our friends across the border have. Found it in Arvika – double-parked outside a supermarket. Double-parked and with a lady's handbag on the seat. Full of the usual junk, you know – powder compact, comb, all that sort of stuff. Driving licence, too. *And* a couple of credit cards. Shouldn't take long to trace who owns it. One of my lads is on to it now.'

A feeble 'Oh?' was all Lessner was able to manage before the inspector went on: 'The Swedes drove your car to the border and we picked it up there. The forsenic boys'll have to give it a good going-over first – prints, you know, things like that – then you can have it back. It's all in one piece, so don't worry.'

'Well, thank you,' Curt Lessner said, clearing his throat. 'Strange that someone should leave a handbag in it, though, isn't it?' he ventured.

'The woman who took your car did more than leave her bag behind,' Inspector Svendsen answered. 'On the way to Arvika she stopped at a café. Anders', it's called. Just the other side of the border. Had a snack. Well, a dinner, actually. Meat and veg and all the trimmings. Anyway, somehow she managed to break a sauceboat. Sauce all over the place, the manager said. Most of it went on to the sofa, I gather. Nothing on her, apparently. The manager took it in his stride, but she was awfully put out, it seems – wanted to pay for the damage and getting the sofa cleaned. In the end she left her card so that they could contact her when they knew what it came to. So there you are: we've had it handed to us on a plate, so to speak.' The inspector laughed heartily at his own joke.

'But how did you find all this out so quickly?' Lessner asked. 'That she'd stopped at a café, I mean.'

'Simple. The bill from Anders' was in her bag. Dated the same day. The Swedish police checked with the café, and there you are.'

'But if you know that much, then you must know her name as well. I mean to say, driving licence and all that…'

'Of course we do,' the policeman agreed. 'It's no secret. Lillen Aas. Lillen Johanne Aas, to be exact. Lives in Skippergaten, out at Nordstrand. Number twenty-two. Three-roomed flat. Very nice too, I hear. Not my department, actually, but I sent one of our cars up to have a look. There was no one home. Never mind, she's bound to turn up soon. And when she does we'll let you know.'

'Lillen Aas?' Curt Lessner stammered. 'But she's my secretary! She's been off work for a few days – since Monday, in fact. But it's only been two days since my car disappeared…'

'Nothing very strange about that,' said the inspector. 'She could have taken your car without showing up for work, couldn't she? Did you ever lend it to her, by the way?'

'Yes, sometimes. Odd errands for the office, you know.'

'Will you be wanting to take the matter further, Mr Lessner?' the inspector asked. 'Prosecute, that is.'

'Er, er…I don't know.' Lessner made an effort to pull himself together. 'I suppose I ought to, really. But Lillen…Do I have to decide that now?' he asked.

'No, Mr Lessner,' the inspector reassured him. 'There's plenty of time for that.'

Curt Lessner thanked him and put the phone down. His mind reeling, he buried his face in his hands. Lillen – Lill – couldn't possibly have stolen his car. Nor could she have broken a sauceboat in a café in Sweden.

People who're dead don't steal cars. They don't steal anything.

And Lillen Aas *was* dead.

He'd killed her himself.

Everything had gone so well until Lill entered his life.

Blonde, petite, with eyes of speedwell blue, one day she had walked blithely into his office to apply for the vacant post of secretary in the small charter business and travel agency he had opened barely three years earlier.

'I haven't many references, I'm afraid,' she'd said with a disarming smile. 'On the other hand I learn fast.'

She was twenty-six. A woman, but a woman who, outwardly at least, had somehow retained the naïveté of a child.

'Can you type?'

'Yes. Not all that fast, but I'm pretty accurate. I have it taped, in other words.'

'"Taped"?' he'd mused. Strange expression for a girl as young as she was to use.

Later he had come to realise that she was full of contradictions like that.

She was right about learning fast.

She did. Very fast.

Annie hadn't liked her at all – understandably. Having been married to her Curt for twenty-odd years, she soon tumbled to the fact that he was up to something. Or, rather, that *they* were. And she'd been right. Only three nights later he and his new secretary found themselves in bed together.

After that there was no going back, at least not for him.

He had misjudged her completely. Taken it for granted that she'd jump at a chance to get into the racket. Earn a small fortune and then perhaps in a few years, when they'd stashed enough away, decamp to the Caribbean. Both of them. Settle down and enjoy life in a country where prices were more reasonable than in Norway and where a person could bask in the sunshine all year round instead of spending half the time frozen to the marrow. The plan was simplicity itself. All she had to do was act as a courier. Take parties of tourists over, show them around, and bring them back. Only in her luggage on the return trip there was always a wad or two of brightly coloured tourist brochures, tightly held by elastic bands. Nothing strange about that. If she were ever asked, she had only to say that they needed them to help make brochures of their own in Norwegian. But she never *was* asked – which was just as well, since a small space cut out in the middle of each bundle was packed tight with cocaine.

After three trips Lill had suddenly called a halt. She wanted out. She had earned enough to make her comfortable, and what was more, she had fallen for one of the pilots on the Rio run. So that was that.

'But what about me?' he'd protested, his whole world suddenly shattered.

'You? You'll be all right. You're not exactly short of money, are you? And as for you-know-what, well – you have your Annie. You *are* married, you know. Besides, you're twenty years older than I am, don't forget. Twenty. That's eighteen too many as far as I'm concerned.'

If only she'd not brought up the difference in their ages! Or not smiled so...condescendingly. Pityingly, almost. She'd made him feel practically senile.

That was why he'd killed her. Not that he'd meant to.

Before he realised it he'd lashed out at her and caught her a glancing blow behind the ear with the flat of his hand. It had sent her reeling, and as she fell her head struck the corner of his desk with a dull thud. Even now he wasn't sure whether it was he or the desk that had killed her. What he did know was that she was undeniably dead. She'd just crumpled up on the floor and lain staring up at him with sightless blue eyes until finally, unable to bear it any longer, he'd steeled himself to close them.

Aghast at what he'd done, he'd sat down for a moment to consider his next move. Strangely enough, there didn't seem to be any blood, and it was that that had encouraged him to try to get away with it. The point was: how?

Obviously he had to get the body out of his office without being seen. Now, right away. It was already getting late – which fortunately meant that it was dark.

That was probably why he'd managed it.

But *had* he managed it? It was all beginning to seem unreal.

After the inspector's phone call he sat quietly for a while, trying to steady his nerves. Then he locked up the office and drove home in the car he'd hired in place of his own. As soon as he got in he strode across to the drinks cabinet in the living-room and poured himself a stiff measure of whisky. Gulping it down almost in one, he seated himself at the window and stared out into the night.

Before him lay the garden, but all he saw was the place where Lill's body lay, deep in some undergrowth, well off the beaten track.

'What's wrong, Curt?' his wife asked sharply, entering the room from the kitchen. 'You've been acting so strangely lately. What's got into you?'

'The police phoned,' he answered, his face averted. 'Just before I left. They've found the car. Across the border in Arvika. Lillen's handbag was on the seat. There were some other things, too ...'

'That hussy!' his wife burst out. 'A hussy and a thief, that's what she is! It doesn't surprise me in the least. I've known it all along. Well, it'll put a stop to your fun and games, that's one good thing.'

'Don't talk like that, Annie,' her husband said thickly. 'There's never been anything between us. I've told you so before. All I've ever done is to defend her when you kept on running her down. Anyway, I don't think *she* took the car. More likely someone else who wanted to hurt her for some reason.'

'There you go again, defending her! If she didn't steal the car, why hasn't she shown a sign of life? Reported her handbag missing? She's bound to have had something in it more important than a compact and a lipstick. Women always do these days. Credit cards, that kind of thing. Oh, no, this time she's gone too far! Just wait till I see her again, I'll tell her a thing or two, believe you me! She can't twist *me* round her little finger, the way she can you.'

Curt Lessner looked at his wife without answering. Suddenly he rose to his feet and stumbled to the bathroom. He reached it just in time to be sick into the wash-basin.

He knew Lill was dead. And the dead don't steal.

Or break sauceboats.

Later that night he was taken really ill. He felt feverish and several times he found himself in the bathroom again, trying to be sick. Only now the sole result was a heaving stomach and a dry rasp in his throat.

'You can't go on like this Curt,' his wife said. 'We shall have to get the doctor.' They were the first kind words she'd spoken to him for a long time, he reflected sadly. Ever since Lillen Aas had come into his life, in fact.

'It'll pass,' he assured her. 'I'll be all right in the morning you'll see. I must have had something that's disagreed with me.'

His wife gave him a searching look but held her peace.

As he lay tossing and turning, unable to sleep, he realised that she too was awake. His brain was in a whirl. What on earth was he to do? He was certain that Lill was dead. But dead people didn't steal cars, he reasoned yet again. Or spill sauce on sofas…

Shortly before nine next morning he phoned the inspector and told him – which was true enough – that he thought the whole story of the car theft had something fishy about it. 'Why should she leave her bag on the seat?' he asked. 'And how did she come to break the sauceboat? Sounds crazy to me. Do you have a description of her? The people at the café must remember what she looked like.'

'All I know is that she was blonde and looked very young. Childlike, the manager said. But I can phone the police in Arvika and ask if they know any more, if you like,' the policeman offered.

'No don't bother,' Curt Lessner said hastily. 'There's no need for that. It's just that it all seems so strange to me. I mean, she only had to ask me and I'd have let her have the car anyway. She must have known that…'

'Just a moment,' the inspector broke in. 'Hang on a sec, will you?' Curt Lessner heard him lay the receiver aside and walk away. A minute or so later he returned and said: 'It seems that the car was full of Lillen Johanne Aas's finger prints. So there we are – it must have been her who drove it to Arvika.'

'Oh, well – yes, I see. That settles it, then, doesn't it?' Curt Lessner said lamely, hurrying to replace the receiver before it fell from his hand.

While he was shaving he studied his face in the mirror. 'God,' he thought to himself, 'I look like death warmed up.' He shuddered as the grotesque aptness of the expression suddenly struck him. At breakfast he gave up after a tentative bite of toast.

'Stay at home, Curt,' his wife urged him. 'You can't go to the office in that state. It's Saturday, anyway. And I'd be a darned sight happier if you'd let the doctor have a look at you.'

'Nonsense,' her husband replied irritably. 'Of course I'm going. Place doesn't run itself, you know.'

He changed his mind, however, when he realised that Annie was going into town. If he really had been having hallucinations, he had better find out straightaway. And the only way to do that was to go back to where he had hidden Lill's body and make sure.

If only none of it had ever happened! 'Oh, God,' he thought to himself, 'let it all be in my mind!' But somehow he knew that it wasn't.

He felt he would give anything to be able to see Lill again. Just to see her – alive! She could marry anyone she liked. He'd never trouble her again. No other woman, either. He'd learnt his lesson. Dear, dear Lill…

As soon as his wife was safely out of the house he took the hire car and drove the same route he had taken on that fateful night with Lill's body lying crumpled up under a blanket on the back seat. Her last drive. It *must* have been.

He stopped the car at the same place as last time. Nerving himself, he opened the door and half-walked, half-ran to the thicket into which he had thrust the body.

Stumbling into the midst of it, he parted the bushes and peered into the shadows. The body was exactly where he had left it.

At that moment he heard the sound of footsteps crashing though the bushes behind him.

It was the police.

First to arrive on the scene was Inspector Svendsen, the policeman he'd spoken to on the phone. Just behind him Curt Lessner glimpsed the trim figure of a woman. The inspector introduced her: Detective Sergeant Sylvia Larsgaard.

'I realised as soon as Lill disappeared that something serious must have happened to her. She loved that flat of hers. It was almost part of her. She'd never have gone off and left it like that. She told me once that she knew something about you that could ruin you for life, only she never said what it was. As the days went by, I got to thinking about what she'd said. That's what made me take your car. I thought that if you'd killed her and I could fix it so that it seemed she was still alive – well, with a bit of luck you'd feel you had to go back and see. She had the other key, remember? I found it on her dressing-table. And – well, it worked, didn't it?'

Detective Sergeant Sylvia Larsgaard. Blonde, petite, eyes like speedwells. Four or five years older than Lill, but even so the very image of her sister.

ELLA GRIFFITHS

4 Post-reading activity on *The Dead Don't Steal*

Speaking and listening *Improvised press conference*

a **In a group**, improvise the press conference that takes place after Curt's arrest, trial and conviction for the murder of Lillen Aas.

b One member of your group plays the part of Inspector Svendsen and another takes on the role of Lillen's sister. The rest are journalists on various Norwegian newspapers. The journalists' task is to question Inspector Svendsen and Lillen's sister, who must answer in role.

c The journalists should draw up a list of questions to put to the police at the press conference; for example, 'How did you start setting up the situation that drew Curt Lessner into your net?' They should do this together. The people playing the parts of Inspector Svendsen and Lillen's sister should prepare by referring back to the story and working out the questions they are likely to be asked.

d Bear in mind as you prepare this improvisation that Lillen's murder is a really 'big' news story. One paper, for instance, has already prepared a front-page headline:

Bergen police solve mystery murder of travel agent's secretary

e When everyone in your group is ready, act out the press conference.

5 Text focus

Reading for understanding

a **In a group**, find evidence from the story that the police catch Curt Lessner by using 'psychological warfare' (that is, by playing on his mind) rather than by more normal means. Discuss in particular:

- the information Inspector Svendsen gives Curt on the phone, and the *tone* in which he gives it.
- the way in which Curt feels increasingly unwell as the story goes on.
- the reasons why Curt feels he *has* to return to the spot where he has hidden Lillen's body.

b **As a class**, discuss Curt's motives for murdering Lillen. In your view, to what extent does the writer:

- present Lillen in a sympathetic light?
- make us feel that Curt has good reasons for killing her?

c **By yourself**, write on the following topic:

'Explain how the police pressurize Curt Lessner into giving himself away. In your opinion, is there anything he could have done to avoid capture – and, if so, what?'

Reading and response

d **As a class**, or **in groups**, consider two aspects of Ella Griffith's story-telling technique by discussing the questions which follow:

Characterisation

Writers can present their characters to us in different ways. For example, characters can tell their own stories in the first person, or they can be described by the writer in the third person.

Discuss the different ways in which the following characters are portrayed in *The Dead Don't Steal*:

- Inspector Svendsen.
- Lillen Aas.
- Curt.

Flashback

(i) What do you understand by the term 'flashback' as a story-telling technique? Think of examples from films and from other novels and stories you have read.

(ii) In *The Dead Don't Steal*, the middle part of the story takes the form of a flashback, beginning with 'Everything had gone so well…' (page 22) and ending 'It was all beginning to seem unreal.' (page 24).

(iii) Put forward your views on why Ella Griffiths has included this flashback section. Would your response to the story have been different without it?

e **By yourself,** write briefly about the part played in this story by Curt's wife, Annie. For what reasons do you think she is important to the story as a whole?

6 Written activities linked to both stories

By yourself, write on one or more of the following topics:

a Describe Mrs Werle's next murder. Use the knowledge you have gained from *The Sweet Old Lady Who Cried Wolf* about Mrs Werle's:

- character and background.
- motives for committing the murders.
- methods of covering her tracks.

Write in the first person, as if you are the old lady herself. This means that your style of writing will be different from the third-person style of Mari Waagaard's story.

b Imagine you are Inspector Svendsen. Write your case notes and your official report on how the Bergen police proved that Curt Lessner had murdered his secretary.

When planning, look back over *The Dead Don't Steal* to make sure that you cover all the details of the police investigation. Write in a suitable form. Your style should be as clear and concise as possible.

c Look back to Activity 1. Put yourself in the place of the teenager suspected of burgling the old couple's house.

The police have agreed not to press charges if you write to the Superintendent of the local CID giving evidence to prove beyond doubt that you cannot possibly be guilty.

Plan and draft carefully what you are going to say, then write your letter. It will need to be formal in style and in the way it is laid out.

d You have pulled off the 'perfect' crime. Explain how you did it in a series of secret diary entries.

You will need to bring out:

- the nature of the crime and your motive(s) for committing it.
- how you planned both the crime and your alibi.
- how you managed to avoid suspicion and capture.

The crime you choose to describe is entirely up to you, as long as it sounds convincing. Write at least four separate diary entries.

7 End-of-Unit written assignments

Write on one or more of the following titles. Refer closely to the stories to back up your ideas and comments.

Subject-matter and themes

a Compare the two murderers in these stories – Mrs Werle and Curt Lessner. One 'gets away with it' but the other one does not. Explain why.

b Describe how the title of each story applies to what happens in it. Say, with reasons, whether or not you feel the titles are well chosen.

Story-telling techniques

c Both stories rely a great deal on suspense for their effectiveness. Show how the suspense is built up in each case. Do you think one story is more successful than the other in keeping us guessing?

d 'Ella Griffiths takes us much deeper into Curt's mind than Mari Waagaard takes us into Mrs Werle's.'

Show this to be true by comparing the way the two characters concerned are presented to us. Why do you think each writer has chosen a different way of portraying her central character?

General

e Do you agree with the following description of both stories:

'*The Sweet Old Lady Who Cried Wolf* shows a murderer successfully outwitting the police, whereas *The Dead Don't Steal* shows the police successfully outwitting a murderer'?

In the light of your decision, say which story you find more effective as a tale of murder.

UNIT TWO

FAMILIES

The Examination Result

Alun Williams

The Examination Result is about a boy who takes an important examination. He has to wait anxiously for the result, having been made aware by his family of the importance of passing it – not only for himself, but also for them.

The Breadwinner

Leslie Halward

The Breadwinner is about a boy who has just started work. His father is unemployed and his mother is struggling to make ends meet. Both are eager to make use of their son's first week's wages.

1 Pre-reading activity on *The Examination Result*

Speaking and listening *Role-play*

With a partner, rehearse and role-play the following situations:

Situation 1

A is 15 years old. **B** is his or her parent. The annual school report has just been delivered. It is not a good one. It contains statements like:

Science
A has had a disappointing year. Although s/he seems quite interested in class, homework has often been rushed and, in some cases, not finished. In End-of-Unit tests, A has gained lower marks than I would have expected.

English
A's creative writing is highly promising and s/he makes intelligent comments in class. However, A must really buckle down to some hard work in literature essays next year if s/he is to gain good grades in the GCSE examination.

B continues to read through the report. **A** tries to explain why the various teachers' comments are exaggerated or unfair.

How will this conversation end?

Situation 2

A is a student who has just received his or her GCSE results. **B** is his or her parent. The results are surprising and disappointing to both of them. **A** needed at least five grade Cs or above to progress into the sixth form or go to college. S/he has actually got only two such grades: one Grade A and one Grade C. The rest are all Ds and Es.

What went wrong? What can be done about it? How will **A**'s future plans be affected? **B**, the parent, is devastated but tries to be comforting.

How will this situation resolve itself?

Now read *The Examination Result*

THE EXAMINATION RESULT

Happened about thirty years ago. I was eleven. We were just the five brothers at home: Cornelius, Emlyn, Emrys, Edwin and myself. My mother had died when I was two and I remembered nothing of her. There was no photograph of her in the house. My father, during the three years he survived, had destroyed them all to blunt the stab of recollection.

Cornelius had started a small business and by means of working from dawn to midnight was doing quite well. Cornelius was a very bright lad. He had won a scholarship to the Grammar School, but had been unable to take it up because mother's illness ate up the money in the house and made my father ignore everything except her.

This fact had a curious effect on Cornelius. He saw it as the chief defeat of his life and he made sure that Emrys, Emlyn and Edwin won their scholarships and made their way to the Grammar School. But it was on me that he centred his greatest hopes. He said that we four would blaze a trail of glory through the Grammar School with me providing the brightest flames at the rear, the last and best.

Each evening after work or at slack periods during the hours when I helped him in the shop he checked on the state of my English and arithmetic. He brought me a little library of good books and saw that I read them. 'I'm willing to work in that shop,' he would say. 'For you I would work right through the night, clean the floor of the potato shed with my own body, but don't let me down, any of you. That's all I ask.' His eyes would settle, green and intense, on me. 'You especially.'

And so we came to the spring of the year in which I was to sit the scholarship examination for Grammar School. The golden weather came soon that year and Cornelius kept me back from the lovely beckoning slopes on which I wanted to play with my friends.

'Time for that later,' he said. 'I do without things I want, a lot of things. So can you with a prize like that at stake.' I can still see the strain and sadness on his face as he said that. I heard later that he told the girl he was friendly with that he would not marry until I, the youngest of the brothers, had completed a course at the University, ten or eleven years to go. She said she could not wait so long and left him.

I got wound up with anxiety a week before the examination. I had violent stomach cramp. At school I would sit without a word in the corner of the concrete-covered yard, not even lifting my head when my friends crowded round me and told me to stop being moody. I said nothing about this to Cornelius in case he might think I was making excuses in advance.

On the day of the examination, every inch of my being was in a turmoil. The pain got right into the nib and made it blunder foolishly. I made every

mistake in arithmetic and spelling within reach. The exam was held in the art room of the Grammar School. The walls were hung with plaster casts of tigers' mouths and human lips, utterly silent and utterly threatening. As I left the room at the end of the afternoon, even the air through which I walked seemed to crumble in ruin.

It was on a Friday that our headmaster, old Mr Robias, ordered the whole school to be brought into the main hall. He said the school had had a triumph. We had twice as many pupils on the list as any other school in the area.

He read out the names. My senses picked up every speck of sensation as the loud, proud baritone voice boomed out its message. My name was not called.

I was first out of the hall. I ran alone on to the hillside that rose steeply behind the street in which I lived. I sat down, my back tight against a small wild apple tree that had a hole in it into which my back fitted. It had been mine since early childhood. It was where I went whenever I felt too angry, lost or cheated. My eyes were fixed on the back of our house, on the kitchen door through which Cornelius would pass at a quarter to six when he came home for tea.

I grew hungry. When Cornelius came into sight and put his hand on the latch of the kitchen door it had the effect on me of a summons. I got up and made my way down to the house, my mind and heart empty of everything except my fear.

When I went in, my brothers were seated at the table, eating in silence. Not one of them looked up as I came in. I sat on my chair. There were pockets of thunder in all four corners of the kitchen. I was excited by the sight of food but my fingers could not bring themselves to approach it.

'Well?' said Cornelius.

'I didn't pass,' I said. I wanted to run, but my legs had worked themselves round the legs of the chair and would not budge.

Cornelius stood up and threw his knife and fork on the plate with a terrifying clatter. He leaned over and hit my face with his full strength. The blow toppled me off the chair. I heard a few vague little sounds of protest from Emrys, Emlyn and Edwin. I shouted something angry, a formless childish oath that caught up a thousandth of the rage and bewilderment I felt.

Cornelius raised his arm again, but I slithered along the floor and shot my hand up to the latch of the door. The iron latch had been worn thin and sharp by age and use. I felt it cut my skin. But the door opened and out I rushed. No one followed.

ALUN WILLIAMS

2 Post-reading activity on *The Examination Result*

Speaking and listening *Hot-seating Cornelius*

a **In a group**, put Cornelius in the 'hot seat'. Your purpose is to explore his attitudes and his motives for behaving towards Alun in the way he does.

b One member of your group acts as Cornelius. He must answer in character while everyone else questions him about his actions.

c Between you, draw up a list of about five questions. For example:

- Why was it so important to you that Alun passed his scholarship exam?
- Looking back, don't you think you put too much pressure on Alun as the exam drew near?

d Whoever is acting Cornelius needs time to prepare his answers to the completed list of questions by looking back at the story.

e Hold your hot-seat session. Appoint someone to note down briefly what Cornelius says.

f Finish this activity by contributing to a **class discussion** in which you consider these questions:

- Does Cornelius really believe he is acting in Alun's best interests? How do you know?
- If you had been in Cornelius's place, would you have treated Alun differently – and, if so, how?

3 Text focus

Reading for understanding

a **In a group**, re-read the relevant parts of the story and say what impressions they give you of Alun's feelings when:

- Cornelius makes him study hard before the exam takes place.
- he is in the art room actually sitting the exam.

- he is listening to Mr Robias read out the names of those who have passed.

- Cornelius hits him across the face.

- he rushes out of the kitchen at the end of the story.

b There are only three occasions on which Cornelius speaks during the whole story. **With a partner**, find them and re-read them aloud, using a suitable tone of voice. Then discuss what they tell you about:

- Cornelius's view of himself as head of the family.

- the effect on Cornelius of being unable to take up his own scholarship to the Grammar School.

c **As a class**, discuss the five alternative titles for the story listed below. How far do you find each of them appropriate to its themes?

- Breaking Free
- The Chief Defeat of his Life
- The Death of Childhood
- A Family Failing
- Frustrations

Reading and response

d **As a class**, or **in groups**, consider three aspects of Alun Williams's story-telling technique by discussing the questions which follow:

Viewpoint

The story is told in the first person and the viewpoint throughout is that of Alun himself. For what reasons do you think the writer chooses to tell the story in this way? Would it have made any difference if we had seen the events through Cornelius's eyes?

Setting

There are four main settings in the story – the 'lovely beckoning slopes' of the surrounding countryside; the art room in the Grammar School; the hillside with its 'small wild apple tree'; and the family kitchen.

Describe the atmosphere of each of these settings, bringing out the main differences between them. What do they contribute to the story as a whole? They have been said to fulfil a *symbolic* function. Can you find any evidence to support this view?

Dialogue

There is very little dialogue in the story. Do you think this adds to, or detracts from, its effectiveness?

e **By yourself**, choose an alternative title for *The Examination Result* – either one of those on the previous page or one of your own.

Write an account of how your chosen title sums up the story's main themes and indicates the way in which they are conveyed to us.

4 Written activities linked to *The Examination Result*

By yourself, write on one or more of the following topics:

a Imagine that Alun returns home later the same evening. Cornelius and his brothers are all in the house. Describe what happens. *Either* use the same story form as the one you have read, writing as if you are Alun, *or* write it as a playscript.

Concentrate on bringing out Alun's feelings and the attitudes of his four brothers, including Cornelius's. How will the story end?

b Use the title *The Examination Result* for a piece of writing based on your own experience. Write about any kind of exam or test you have taken, not necessarily in school.

How did you prepare? What were your feelings before, during and after taking it? How did you find out the result and what were your reactions and those of other interested parties – your family, your teacher (or coach), your friends, etc?

c A recent newspaper article appeared under the headline 'More Exams for Secondary Pupils'. It argued, among other things, that:

- frequent testing in school ensures that standards remain high.
- examinations are a vital preparation for adult life.
- parents need more reliable information about their children's progress than they get from school reports alone.

Write a letter to the newspaper giving your own views about regular examinations.

d Write a real or imagined story based on a young person who fails to live up to their family's high expectations. The story can deal with any subject you wish. Write it in normal story form, as a series of diary entries, or entirely in dialogue.

5 Pre-reading activity on *The Breadwinner*

Speaking and listening *Dilemmas!*

a **In a group**, read the four scenarios below. Imagine you are faced with the dilemmas they describe.

Dilemma 1

You have promised to be back home from a mid-week party by 11 pm You return after midnight. Do you:

- say you were enjoying yourself so much that you simply forgot the time?
- argue that your friends' parents allow *their* sons and daughters to stay out late, so yours should too?
- tell a lie (for example, say your money was stolen so you had to walk home instead of catching the last bus)?

Dilemma 2

Your parents have banned you from dressing in the latest teenage fashion. Do you:

- keep the 'banned' clothes at a friend's house and change there when you go out?
- gradually try to persuade your parents that everyone's wearing it and you'll be left out unless *you* do?
- get out the family photo album and remind your parents that *they* dressed trendily when they were fashion-conscious teenagers?

Dilemma 3

During a blazing row, one of your parents hits you. This is completely out of character. Do you:

- storm out of the house, saying you'll stay with your best friend's family until things cool off?
- refuse to accept their apology and sulk for days in order to make them feel even more guilty?
- say you're sorry for causing the row and admit that you deserved what you got?

Dilemma 4

Your parents have been arguing with each other for weeks. Both are encouraging you to take sides. Do you:

- refuse to get involved and tell them to sort out their own problems by themselves?
- decide which parent you feel most sympathy with and join in on their side?
- try to restore harmony by saying that their constant bickering is upsetting you?

b For each dilemma, say which of the three alternative courses of action you would take and fully explain why. If other members of your group choose differently from you, ask them to justify their decisions.

Now read *The Breadwinner*

THE BREADWINNER

The parents of a boy of fourteen were waiting for him to come home with his first week's wages.

The mother had laid the table and was cutting some slices of bread and butter for tea. She was a little woman with a pinched face and a spare body, dressed in a blue blouse and skirt, the front of the skirt covered with a starched white apron. She looked tired and frequently sighed heavily.

The father, sprawling inelegantly in an old armchair by the fireside, legs outstretched, was little too. He had watery blue eyes and a heavy brown moustache, which he sucked occasionally.

These people were plainly poor, for the room, though clean, was meanly furnished, and the thick pieces of bread and butter were the only food on the table.

As she prepared the meal, the woman from time to time looked contemptuously at her husband. He ignored her, raising his eyebrows, humming or tapping his teeth now and then with his finger-nails, making a pretence of being profoundly bored.

'You'll keep your hands off the money,' said the woman, obviously repeating something that she had already said several times before. 'I know what'll happen to it if you get hold of it. He'll give it to me. It'll pay the rent and buy us a bit of food, and not go into the till at the nearest public-house.'

'You shut your mouth,' said the man, quietly.

'I'll not shut my mouth!' cried the woman, in a quick burst of anger. 'Why should I shut my mouth? You've been boss here for long enough. I put up with it when you were bringing money into the house, but I'll not put up with it now. You're nobody here. Understand? *Nobody*. I'm boss and he'll hand the money to me!'

'We'll see about that,' said the man, leisurely poking the fire.

Nothing more was said for about five minutes.

Then the boy came in. He did not look older than ten or eleven years. He looked absurd in long trousers. The whites of his eyes against his black face gave him a startled expression.

The father got to his feet.

'Where's the money?' he demanded.

The boy looked from one to the other. He was afraid of his father. He licked his pale lips.

'Come on now,' said the man. 'Where's the money?'

'Don't give it to him,' said the woman. 'Don't give it to him, Billy. Give it to me.'

The father advanced on the boy, his teeth showing in a snarl under his big moustache.

'Where's the money?' he almost whispered.

The boy looked him straight in the eyes.

'I lost it,' he said.

'You – *what*?' cried his father.

'I lost it,' the boy repeated.

The man began to shout and wave his hands about.

'Lost it! *Lost it*! What are you talking about? How could you lose it?'

'It was in a packet,' said the boy, 'a little envelope. I lost it.'

'Where did you lose it?'

'I don't know. I must have dropped it in the street.'

'Did you go back and look for it?'

The boy nodded. 'I couldn't find it,' he said.

The man made a noise in his throat, half grunt, half moan – the sort of noise that an animal would make.

'So you lost it, did you?' he said. He stepped back a couple of paces and took off his belt – a wide, thick belt with a heavy brass buckle. 'Come here,' he said.

The boy, biting his lower lip so as to keep back the tears, advanced, and the man raised his arm. The woman, motionless until that moment, leapt forward and seized it. Her husband, finding strength in his blind rage, pushed her aside easily. He brought the belt down on the boy's back. He beat him unmercifully about the body and legs. The boy sank to the floor, but did not cry out.

When the man had spent himself, he put on the belt and pulled the boy to his feet.

'Now you'll get off to bed,' he said.

'The lad wants some food,' said the woman.

'He'll go to bed. Go and wash yourself.'

Without a word the boy went into the scullery and washed his hands and face. When he had done this he went straight upstairs.

The man sat down at the table, ate some bread and butter and drank two cups of tea. The woman ate nothing. She sat opposite him, never taking her eyes from his face, looking with hatred at him. Just as before, he took no notice of her, ignored her, behaved as if she were not there at all.

When he finished the meal he went out.

Immediately he had shut the door the woman jumped to her feet and ran upstairs to the boy's room.

He was sobbing bitterly, his face buried in the pillow. She sat on the edge of the bed and put her arms about him, pressed him close to her breast, ran her fingers through his disordered hair, whispered endearments, consoling him. He let her do this, finding comfort in her caresses, relief in his own tears.

After a while his weeping ceased. He raised his head and smiled at her, his wet eyes bright. Then he put his hand under the pillow and withdrew a small dirty envelope.

'Here's the money,' he whispered.

She took the envelope and opened it and pulled out a long strip of paper with some figures on it – a ten shilling note and a sixpence.

LESLIE HALWARD

6 Post-reading activity on *The Breadwinner*

Speaking and listening *Improvisation*

a **With a partner**, improvise the conversation between the boy's parents when his father returns home.

Assume that:

- when he first comes in, the father has calmed down somewhat and is prepared to be more reasonable about the money.
- about half-way through the conversation, his wife reveals that Billy has given his wages to her.

b After deciding who will play which part, take about ten minutes to prepare what you are going to say. Do this apart rather than together.

c Try to make your character consistent with what you have learned about him or her from reading the story.

d Finish this activity by holding a **class discussion** in which you describe briefly how your conversation went, particularly the way in which it ended. Did it follow a similar course to that of other pairs – or were there important differences? If so, why?

7 Text focus

Reading for understanding

a **In a group**, re-read the relevant parts of the story and say what impressions they give you of Billy's feelings when:

- his father first asks him to hand over his wage packet.
- he lies to his father.
- his father has finished beating him.
- his mother comes to his room to comfort him.
- he hands the wage packet to his mother.

b **With a partner**, look back over the whole story. Find *one* comment made by each of the three characters which you agree best sums up:

- the relationship between husband and wife.
- the relationship between Billy and his father.
- the relationship between Billy and his mother.

Then **join up with another pair**. Compare and justify your choices. Between you, discuss the tone of voice each character uses as he or she makes the comments you have picked out.

c **As a class**, discuss the reasons the writer may have had for entitling this story *The Breadwinner*.

Reading and response

d **As a class**, or **in groups**, consider three aspects of Leslie Halward's story-telling technique by discussing the questions which follow:

Suspense

(i) How does the writer build up an atmosphere of tension and suspense before Billy returns home?

(ii) How is the feeling of suspense maintained in the final part of the story, after Billy's father has gone out?

Characterisation

(i) The characterisation of the father depends partly on him being compared to an animal. Find as many examples of this as you can. What is the effect of such comparisons?

(ii) How does the writer characterise Billy's mother in such a way that we are made to sympathise with her? Why do you think he wants us to do so?

Dialogue

In the first and last parts of the story there is very little direct speech. By contrast, the middle part of the story is told almost entirely through dialogue. Why do you think the writer has chosen to use dialogue in this way? Do you find it effective?

e **By yourself**, write an account of how the story's title summarises its main themes and the way in which they are conveyed to us. Quote from the text to back up the points you make.

8 Written activities linked to *The Breadwinner*

By yourself, write on one or more of the following topics:

a Imagine that Billy and his mother both keep personal diaries. Write the entries they make at the end of the day on which the story takes place.

Concentrate most on bringing out their deepest, most private feelings. It has been a 'watershed' day for both of them. What will Billy's feelings be about his father? What will his mother's feelings be about her husband? How will each of them now see the future after what has happened?

b Suppose that Billy *had* given his father the wage packet when he was threatened with a beating. Write an alternative version of the story from this point on, using a style as near as possible to Leslie Halward's.

How will his father react? What will Billy's feelings be about giving in to his father? How will the relationship between Billy's parents be affected? How will this version of the story end?

c Most readers of *The Breadwinner* are likely to feel that the lie Billy tells his father is excusable, even admirable, under the circumstances. Is lying ever justified, though, in real life?

Write on this subject in the form of a discussion essay. Try to present a balanced argument. Draw your examples from your own experience, from true stories you've heard about, and, if possible, from the 'wider world'. A good way of preparing for this piece of work is to ask a cross-section of teenagers and adults for their views on the subject, and include them in your essay.

d Write, in playscript or in dialogue form, an account of a family argument which centres on someone of your age. It can be based on a real or imagined experience. If you wish, use one of the dilemmas in Activity 5 (page 39) to give you a storyline.

There is little point in just scripting a 'shouting match'. Your task should be:

- to make clear through dialogue alone what the situation is that has caused the argument.
- to bring out the characters of those involved by what they say and the way they say it.

9 End-of-Unit written assignments

Write on one or more of the following titles. Refer closely to the stories to back up your ideas and comments.

Subject-matter and themes

a Alun and Billy are both in conflict with a member of their family. Explain the reasons for this in each case. With which boy do you feel more sympathy, and why?

b 'Each family is working out its own problems and frustrations through the son. The boys themselves are blameless.' Do you agree? Give careful reasons to support your opinion.

Story-telling techniques

c Show how each writer builds up a strong sense of conflict in these stories. In which story do you feel the conflict is more fully resolved by the end?

d Compare the way in which Cornelius in *The Examination Result* and Billy's father in the *The Breadwinner* are presented to us. In your view, which of these characters are we made to dislike (or to disapprove of) more?

General

e Which story has made the greater impression on you, and for what reasons?

In planning your answer, think in particular about:

- how each boy reacts to the pressure his family puts on him.
- the depth of feeling each writer gets into his story.
- how true-to-life you feel the situations described in *The Examination Result* and *The Breadwinner* actually are.

Make any other points you feel are relevant, and refer, if you wish, to your own experience of family life.

UNIT THREE

HEARTACHES

Love Letters

Kate Walker

Love Letters, set in an Australian high school, tells how a teenage boy goes to unusual lengths to keep his much sought-after girlfriend – 'the fabulous Fleur'.

Sharon, the Ferryman's Daughter

Valerie Thornton

In *Sharon, the Ferryman's Daughter*, a Scottish teenage girl causes astonishment at school by announcing that she has found a boyfriend much older than herself. How has she done it, and will it last? The other girls are determined to find out.

1 Pre-reading activity on both stories

Speaking and listening *Teen themes*

In a group, read the two letters printed below. They come from the Problem Page of a teenage magazine.

> I have a 15-year-old friend who I think has an eating disorder. She's really lost a lot of weight in the last six months. She came to a party recently wearing a cropped top and leggings. Everyone was shocked because she looked like a skeleton.
>
> The problem is, she won't talk about it. At lunchtime, she now goes home and says she eats there, but I think she's lying. No one's seen her eating anything for ages.
>
> We really want to help her. She used to be a great laugh but now she's gone a lot more quiet. She hardly ever joins in our chats and she's never had a steady boyfriend. What's the best thing to do?

> This might sound stupid but it's driving me nearly insane. I'm writing because I can't tell anyone else how I feel about my Dad.
>
> He and my Mum split up ten years ago, when I was six. It wasn't too bad, though. Dad and I became really good friends. We went fishing and to football matches etc. at weekends. I always had great times staying with him in the school holidays.
>
> He got re-married last year, and he's really changed. His new wife, Denise, has two children. Now Dad seems to have more time for them than for me. What's worse is that Denise is brilliant at making me feel at home when I'm with them. I'm starting to like her better than Mum, who's found herself a pig of a boyfriend called (would you believe) Henry.
>
> Should I ask if I can move in with my Dad?

In your group, talk about:

- your impressions of the teenagers who wrote the letters.
- any experiences which you (or people you know) have had in common with those the writers describe.
- how you think the magazine should reply to each letter, giving helpful and serious advice.

Now read *Love Letters*

LOVE LETTERS

My name's Nick and my chick's name's Fleur. And she has a friend called Helen who's got a boyfriend named Clive. Now this Clive is really weird. Well, he does one weird thing I know of anyway: he writes three-page letters to his girlfriend, Helen, *every* day.

'What's wrong with the nerd?' I asked Fleur. She'd spent a whole lunch time telling me about him.

'There's nothing *wrong* with him,' she said. 'You're so unromantic, Nick.'

'Of course I'm not unromantic!' I said, and I offered her a lick of my ice cream to prove it. She groaned and pulled her PE bag over her head. She didn't want to talk to me any more.

When girls go quiet, that's a bad sign!

'What's wrong?' I asked her.

'You don't love me,' she said.

'Of course I love you,' I told her. I offered her my whole ice cream. She wouldn't take it.

'You don't love me *enough*,' she said.

'How much is *enough*?'

How much ice cream did it take?

'You don't write *me* letters like Clive does to Helen,' she said.

'I don't need to, I see you every day in Computers,' I said. '*And* Chemistry.'

'Clive sees Helen every day in Biology, and Textiles, and Home Science, and assembly, and roll call,' she said, 'and he writes letters to *her*!'

I knew what was happening here: my girlfriend was cooling on me.

'OK,' I said, 'I'll write you a letter.'

'Aw, Nick!' She whipped her PE bag off her head.

I was glad I'd weakened. Fleur is really gorgeous. I couldn't risk losing her for the sake of a few lines scrawled on a piece of paper. I'm the envy of the boys' locker room, having her for a girlfriend.

I sat down that night and began my first letter: 'Dear Fleur…' Then I stared at the page for the next half hour. What do you write in letters to someone you see every day? I chewed my pencil; I chewed my nails. Then, in desperation, I finally asked Mum.

'Write about the things you have in common,' Mum said, so I wrote the following: 'Wasn't that computer class on Tuesday a ROAR? The best bit was when Brando tilted the computer to show us the little button underneath and the monitor fell off.'

I wrote about the Chemistry class too, though it wasn't quite as interesting. Not a single kid muffed their experiment and blew their eyebrows off. But then I got really creative at the end of the letter and added a postscript written in Basic.

I got the letter back next day with 'five-and-a-half out of twenty' marked on the bottom.

'What was wrong with it?' I asked Fleur.

'You made a lot of spelling mistakes for one thing,' she said.

'I was being *myself*!' I told her.

'I didn't notice,' she said. 'You didn't say anything *personal* in it!'

Is that what she wanted, a *personal* letter?

I thought it over for five minutes. There were guys all round the lunch area just waiting to take my place and share their chocolate milk with the fabulous Fleur. If revealing a few personal secrets was what it took to keep her, I could do it.

'Dear Fleur…' I began the second letter that night, 'This is not something I'd tell everyone, but I use a deodorant. Only on sports day or in really hot weather of course.'

No, that was too personal. I ripped up the page and started again. 'Dear Fleur, Guess what? Mrs Hessel blew me up in History today for no reason at all. I was embarrassed to death. Goggle-eyes Gilda laughed her stupid head off.'

Actually, once I'd got started I found the personal stuff not that hard to write. I told Fleur what mark I'd *really* got in the English half-yearlies. Then I told her about a movie I'd seen where this pioneer farming guy loses his plough horse, then loses his wife, then his children, and then his cows get hoof rot. But even though he sits down and bawls his eyes out about it, in the end he walks off into the sunset, a stronger man.

'I'd like to suffer a great personal loss like that,' I told Fleur in the letter, 'and walk away stronger and nobler for it.' Her sole comment on letter number two was: 'You didn't say anything in it about *me*.' And she went off to eat lunch with Helen.

It was time to hit the panic button. Fleur was 'drifting'. I stuffed my sandwiches back in my bag and went looking for Clive. I bailed him up under the stairwell.

'OK, what do you put in your letters to Helen?' I asked him.

Clive turned out to be a decent kid. He not only told me, he gave me a photocopy of the latest letter he was writing to Helen.

You should have seen it!

'Darling Helen, Your hair is like gold. Your eyes remind me of twilight reflected on Throsby Creek. Your ear lobes are…Your eyelashes are…' And so on. It was what you'd call a poetic autopsy.

And as if that wasn't bad enough, he then got into the declarations of love: 'You're special to me because…I yearn for you in History because…I can't eat noodles without thinking of you because…'

'Do girls really go for this sort of thing?' I asked him.

'Helen does,' he said. 'She'd drop me tomorrow if I stopped writing her letters. It's the price you pay if you want to keep your girlfriend.'

So I began my third letter, with Clive's photocopy propped up in front of me as a guide.

'Dear Fleur, Your hair is like…' I began.

Actually, I'd always thought it was like fairy-floss, pretty from a distance but all gooey when you touched it – too much hair-spray, I suppose.

I scrapped that opening and started again.

'Dear Fleur, Your eyes are like…'

Actually, they're a bit small and squinty. I think she might need glasses but she's not letting on.

Scrub the eyes.

'Dear Fleur, Your face is excellent overall. You look like one of those soap-opera dolls.'

I thought I would've been able to go on for hours about her face, but having said that, it seemed to sum her up.

I moved on to the declarations: 'I love you because…' I chewed my pencil again, then my fingernails. This time I couldn't ask Mum.

Why did I love Fleur? Because she was spunky. Because all the guys thought so too. Well, not all of them. Some of them thought she wasn't all that interesting to talk to, but I put that down to jealousy.

Still, I began to wonder, what *had* we talked about in the three weeks we'd been going together? Not much really. She'd never been interested enough in my hockey playing to ask in-depth questions about it. And, I have to admit, I hadn't found her conversation on white ankle boots all that riveting either.

No wonder I was having so much trouble writing letters to her. We had nothing in common. I barely knew her. What were her views on nuclear disarmament? Maybe she didn't have any. Was she pro-Libyan? I didn't know.

I scrapped the letter, scrapped Clive's photocopy, and started again, this time with no trouble at all.

'Dear Fleur, This writing of letters was a very good idea because it gives me the opportunity to say something important to you. I think you're a nice girl and I've enjoyed going steady with you for three weeks but I think we should call it off. Even if it's a great personal loss to both of us, I'm sure we'll walk away stronger and nobler. Yours sincerely, Nick.'

I slipped the letter to her in Computers. She didn't take it too badly, just ripped it up and fed it through the shredder. But then two days later photocopies of my *personal* letter started to circulate the school.

I didn't mind, though, because as a result of that, Goggle-eyes Gilda slipped me a note in History that said, briefly: 'I like your style, Nick. You've got depth.' I took another look at Goggle-eyes. I didn't mind her style either. She has this terrific laugh and she's a whiz on computers.

I wrote back straight away, my own kind of letter this time – honest and to the point: 'Dear Gilda, That three-minute talk you gave on speech day about Third World Famine Relief was really excellent. I'll be eating lunch in the quad if you'd care to join me.'

KATE WALKER

2 Post-reading activity on *Love Letters*

Speaking and listening *Character quadrants*

a **In a group**, discuss what you have learned from the story about its two main characters.

b Record your ideas by filling out a character quadrant for Nick and Fleur. Do it like this:

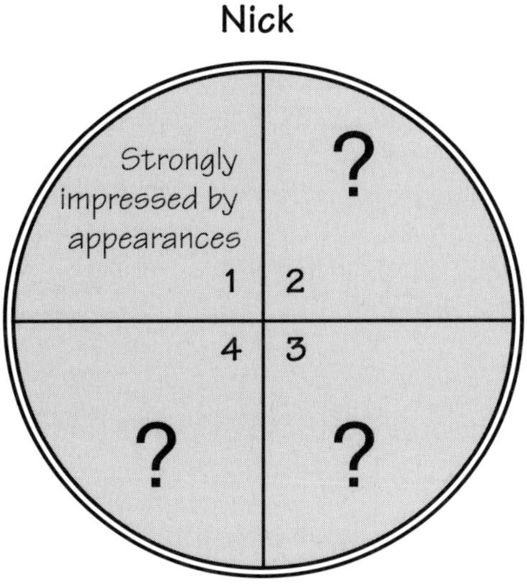

1 I'm the envy of the boys' locker room, having her for a girlfriend.

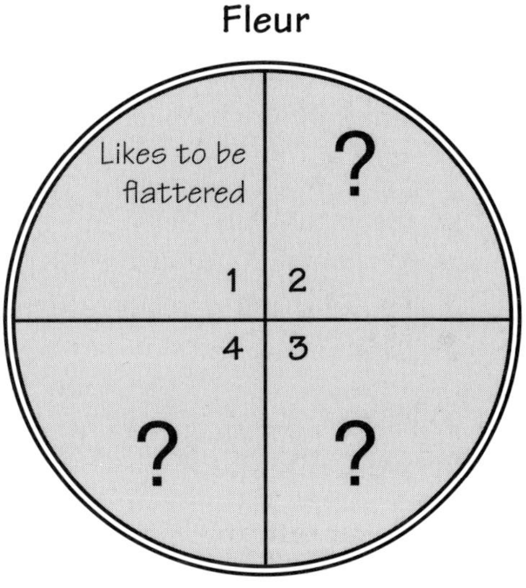

1 'You don't write me letters like Clive does to Helen,' she said.

c Everyone in your group should draw and complete their own quadrant. They need not contain identical points. As you talk, you may find you have different impressions from other people of Nick and Fleur.

d As in the example above, write down a short quotation from the story to illustrate each of your four character points about Nick and Fleur.

e Finish this activity by holding a **class discussion** in which you consider these two questions:

- With which character do you feel more sympathy, and why?
- Which character do you find the more mature, and why?

3 Text focus

Reading for understanding

a **With a partner**, re-read the parts of the story describing Fleur's reactions to the three letters Nick writes her. Discuss whether, in your opinion, her reactions are fair to Nick. Give reasons.

b **As a class**, consider the more serious theme behind Kate Walker's humorous story. Do this by finding the point where Nick says:

'No wonder I was having so much trouble writing letters to her.' (page 51)

Discuss which of the following statements you feel gives the best explanation of why Nick has 'so much trouble' with his love letters:

- He doesn't really like Fleur all that much.
- He is basically a shy person.
- He actually knows very little about what Fleur is like.
- He lacks skill at expressing himself in writing.
- He is too honest.

Whichever statement you think best applies to Nick, find evidence from the story that shows it to be true.

c **By yourself**, write an account of what Nick learns in the course of the story about:

- his relationship with Fleur, *and*
- boy–girl relationships in general.

Reading and response

d **As a class**, or **in groups**, consider three aspects of Kate Walker's story-telling technique by discussing the questions which follow:

Viewpoint

The story is told in the first person ('**My** name's Nick...**I** sat down that night and began **my** first letter.') The viewpoint throughout is Nick's. Why do you think the writer chooses to tell the story in this way? What difference would it have made if we had seen everything through Fleur's eyes?

Letter form

(i) How many letters or 'notes' are actually quoted in the course of the story, and from how many different people?

(ii) Why do you think Kate Walker has based so much of her story on the use of the letter form? Is this device effective? If so, why?

Humour

(i) If *Love Letters* did not amuse its readers, the story would lose much of its appeal. Which parts of it do *you* find funniest?

(ii) How many of the following purposes do you agree are served by the humorous way in which Kate Walker writes:

- To bring out the vanity of both Nick and Fleur?
- To show how teenagers take boy–girl relationships with such deadly seriousness that it can actually be rather funny?
- To make us consider whether some teenagers think so much about appearance that they forget about personality?
- To show how important it is to teenagers to have a girlfriend or boyfriend – and to be *known* to have one?
- To reveal Nick's gradual awareness that he's been going out with Fleur for the wrong reasons?

e **By yourself**, write about Kate Walker's use of humour in the story by giving your response to the following questions:

- Which parts of *Love Letters* do you find most amusing?
- How does the writer's use of humour bring out the story's themes?

4 Written activities linked to *Love Letters*

By yourself, write on one or more of the following topics:

a Write Fleur's reply to Nick's third and final letter. Use your knowledge of the story to express her feelings about:

- how Nick has treated her.
- what she *really* thinks of the letters he has written her.
- the fact that he has now 'finished' with her.

b Look through a selection of teenage magazines. Find and cut out several letters printed in their problem pages. Make sure that they cover a variety of subjects.

Write a personal commentary on the letters you have chosen by sticking them in your book or file and, after each one, describing:

- what they tell you about the *character* of the writer.
- what advice you would give the writer (regardless of any reply that is already printed in the magazine).
- whether you think that the letter is a 'real' one or one which has been 'faked' by the magazine, and your reasons for thinking as you do.

c Write a story which is partly, largely, or entirely based on letters. The number of letter writers you use in the story is for you to decide.

You may write on any subject you wish. Some ideas to consider are:

- The Crime That Went Wrong
- Mistaken Identity
- The Computers Write Back
- Tangled Chain Letters
- The Lost Relative
- Correspondence From The Past

Now read *Sharon, the Ferryman's Daughter*

SHARON, THE FERRYMAN'S DAUGHTER

That she should live on an island in the middle of the river was more than appropriate. Her father was the ferryman. If you wanted to cross the river, you hung a white-painted board on a pair of hooks at the end of the rudimentary pier, then when Sharon's father noticed this, he set out for you in his small boat following a graceful upstream curve to counter the current.

Every morning he rowed his daughter to the shore. But she didn't join the cheerful mob who came to school in the low blue single-decker. Nor did she walk with friends in a chattering swirl of blue uniforms.

Sharon walked alone, by the most direct route, up over the top of the town, past Battlefield Street with the cannons in the middle of it and down along the edge of the George Park towards the school. She would stand alone, her stout walking shoes and thick socks setting her apart from the rest, waiting for the bell.

For all the walking she did, she invariably looked under the weather. She had a long pasty face with a suggestion of spots. Her eyes were pale blue with pale blue National Health glasses, her teeth were long and dirty, and her long hair, which was an unpleasant peachy shade, was greasy and lank as far down as her shoulders.

No one wanted her as their friend. Apart from being inaccessible after school, she had also come late to the school, joining in third year, and her mother was dead. Everyone had established their exclusive cliques and as Sharon wasn't beautiful, they greeted her with studied indifference.

She wasn't victimized as could easily have happened. Just left alone. If you did speak to her, she replied with a whining, nasal voice, speaking softly. She didn't hide behind an assumed dignity, nor was she obviously upset at her situation. She simply accepted her insular position while life flowed around her.

Someone must have been talking to her though, because as soon as it was known that she had found a boyfriend, she became the centre of attention. Her boyfriend was no mere pupil, not even a fifth or sixth year boy for whom many a third year girl longed, but a man. She maintained he was twenty-three. No one was quite sure if it was true or not, so she was cross-questioned in the toilets until everyone was satisfied that she wasn't making it all up.

'And how did you meet him?'

'Walking home from school one day. He asked where I was going, and if he could come with me.'

'What's his name?'

'John.'

'John what?'

'I don't know,' she giggled a little. 'I haven't asked him yet…'

'And what do you do?'

'We go down by the river and walk and hold hands and sometimes we kiss.'

'What's it like?'

She thinks a little, then shrugs her shoulders.

'It's OK. Sometimes he lets me have a puff at his cigarette, but I don't like it very much.'

'Does your Dad know?'

'No, not yet.'

'Are you going to tell him?'

'I don't think so.'

She flashes an uncertain smile with her long yellow teeth. You wonder what sort of man would go with her.

One day she announces they are going to the pictures. Saturday afternoon, so her father won't suspect. No one is sure whether to believe her or not. Afterwards they test her with questions about the cinema, and one girl who's seen the film asks her about the plot.

'I don't remember that bit. We were kissing a lot. One kiss lasted for fifteen whole minutes!'

This was unheard of. She was asked in detail about it.

'Well, he put his hand along the back of the seat, then round here.'

She touches her breast pocket. Those who know about these things nod approvingly.

'Then he sort of pulled me and started kissing me, and just kept on.' She lowers her voice. 'His tongue was there too. But I didn't like that bit very much. It was all slippy.'

The wise ones nod in agreement. She certainly didn't seem to be making it all up. But they wanted proof.

'Why don't you get him to meet you at school? Is he good-looking?'

'I don't know,' she giggles. 'I mean, I could ask him and see what he says…I don't know if you'd think he was good-looking. He's got nice blue eyes and dark brown hair. We just always meet down by the river…'

'Are you going to the pictures again?'

'I don't think so. I'm scared my Dad'll find out. He'd probably kill me.'

One day she says he's going to meet her in the park, after school.

'Go and sit on one of the benches with him so that we can walk past and have a good look at him.'

'I'll try.'

All through the afternoon classes there's an expectant air. The girls in the row by the window look down into the park trying to spot the boyfriend. At four, everyone dithers over their packing up in order to let Sharon out first.

They form small curious groups and several who would have gone for the bus at the school gates decide to walk through the park.

Sharon is sitting on the roundabout, holding hands with a man. She is bursting with pride and self-consciousness. They sweep round in slow circles, displaying themselves to not only Sharon's classmates but to all the other pupils above and below them who also pass homewards through the park.

John seems a bit uncomfortable about being on display. He is unshaven and unkempt. His greasy black hair is lank, in sympathy with Sharon's greasy hair which is the colour of those discoloured tufts around the mouths of white dogs. He wears a dirty blue anorak which fails to conceal a fair-sized beer belly, and he looks old and surly. Nonetheless he's there, with her, and obviously her boyfriend. He decides to leave and tugs her off the roundabout. He takes her away, his arm heavily around her shoulder, her head tilted against his shoulder, awkwardly.

The next day in the toilets everyone is a little reserved. Her pride embarrasses them.

'He's really nice, Sharon!' they gush, and she beams.

'You really look as if you're in love!'

'We are!' she says, her eyes bright. At times she can look almost pretty – if she washed her hair and tried a little eyeshadow.

'He gave me something last night, after school.'

'What?' they chorus with unconcealed curiosity.

'Look!'

She loosens her tie and drags her shirt back from the side of her neck. A livid, bite-shaped bruise nestles there.

'Can you see it? It is still there?'

No one knows what to say.

'Does it hurt?' someone asks.

'A little, but it's quite a nice kind of hurt.'

She fingers it briefly, then covers it up and tightens her tie.

'It's a love bite. It's the first love bite I've ever had!' she says proudly. 'He says he'll give me some more too.'

Sharon is a celebrity.

One day she tells them John has given her love bites all the way down her front. No one is sure whether to believe her or not. Only a few around her throat are visible in PE and she won't reveal the rest.

That afternoon she is called out of class to go and see the headmistress. She can't be in trouble. She's one of the quietest, most biddable pupils in the class.

She comes back much later, her eyes rimmed red, and sniffing. The teacher makes no comment. At the interval they cluster around her in the toilet while she cries openly.

'I don't know what to do,' she rocks herself in misery. No one touches her.

'What happened?'

'She asked to see…I had to undo my blouse, and she saw them all.'

'Was she angry?'

'No not really. She asked if my Dad knew.'

'And he doesn't?'

'No. She said if I didn't stop seeing him she'd tell my Dad.'

'But how does she know?'

'She asked me all about him. I had to tell her,' a sob racked her. 'I don't want to stop seeing John – I love him! She says I'm too young for him, but I'm not! He loves me too, I know, he told me, last night, when he gave me these,' she pressed her hand to her chest. 'I even had a note to get me off swimming, but I forgot it was PE.'

'Did you tell her you would stop seeing him?'

'I had to. But I won't. We'll just have to keep it a secret.'

'When are you seeing him again?'

'Today, after school. Down by the river. He says he's not coming back to the park again,' she laughed a little. 'You've all scared him off.'

'What are you going to tell him?'

'I don't know.'

Sharon was subdued and withdrawn the next day.

'Well, did you see him?'

'Did you tell him?'

'What did he say?'

She smiled quietly and hugged herself.

'He was really nice about it. We went to a place he knew, a sort of hut at the bottom of the fields, and talked about it for ages. He just said it didn't make any difference to us and that he loved me. And he gave me something too, to prove it.'

She hesitates, considering what to say.

'What? More love bites? Where?'

Her demeanour becomes almost withering.

'No, much better.'

'What then?'

A note of hesitancy creeps into the interrogators. A gulf of ignorance is opening between them. Sharon is suddenly wise.

'This!' she decides, holding out her hand. A little silver ring, heart-shaped, is on her middle finger. 'I have to take it off when I go home, but I put it on in bed.'

'It's lovely!' they breathe. But Sharon is beyond them now. Beyond asking. Beyond telling.

The next day she is pale and worried. John wasn't there last night.

'Maybe he's not well. Do you know where he stays?'

'No.'

Nor was he there that evening.

Nor the next.

Sharon would sit in class and twist her ring endlessly while the others retreated from her. She began to be off school, ill, sick. Instead of getting over John she became increasingly morose and would hold herself alone, pale and silent.

Then she stopped coming to school altogether.

Some said her father had found out and wouldn't let her out of his sight. Other said she'd eloped with John. Someone said she'd thrown herself in the river and that her body still hadn't been found. And one girl, much later on, said she'd seen a girl who looked a bit like Sharon pushing a pram.

But that was much later on and by then most of them had forgotten about her.

VALERIE THORNTON

5 Post-reading activity on *Sharon, the Ferryman's Daughter*

Speaking and listening *Truth-testing Sharon*

a **With a partner**, look back through the story together and make a 'truth chart' on which you record evidence that Sharon's account of her relationship with John is true and evidence that she may be inventing some, or all, of it. Make out your chart like this:

True	Invented
She says definitely that her boyfriend's name is John and is certain about his age	When asked about John's surname she can't give an answer – she giggles to hide her confusion
She shows the girls a ring which she says John has given her	There is nothing on the ring to prove it is a love token from John – she could have bought it herself

Try to include up to eight points on your chart.

b **In a group**, question Sharon through role-play. Decide who will take her part and who will be the interviewers. The interview takes place before Sharon disappears from school for ever. It is most important that Sharon is questioned only about things that are mentioned in the story. She must answer in character.

c Finish this activity by taking part in a **class discussion** about whether or not Sharon is telling the whole truth, only part of the truth, or is simply lying about herself and John. Whatever conclusions you come to, consider *all* the reasons she might have for inventing the story of her relationship. Take into account the impressions the story gives us of her.

6 Text focus

Reading for understanding

a **In a group**, trace the way in which the girls' attitudes to Sharon change in the course of the story. Focus on the following points in the plot:

- Before 'it was known that she had found a boyfriend' (page 57).
- After the girls see Sharon and John together in the park and she tells them the next day about her 'love bites' (page 59).
- When Sharon shows them the 'little silver ring' (page 61).
- After Sharon stops coming to school altogether (page 61).

What do you conclude about the nature of the girls' interest in Sharon – and their feelings towards her?

b **With a partner**, look carefully at:

- the physical descriptions of Sharon and John, *and*
- what we learn about their personalities.

Make a list of all the ways in which they are shown to be alike. Why do you think the story draws our attention to the similarities between them?

c **As a class**, consider the sentences listed below. They are from different parts of the story but they are printed in the order in which they appear.

Give your views about why each sentence is important in conveying to us the story's themes:

(i) 'She simply accepted her insular position while life flowed around her.' (page 57).

(ii) 'You wonder what sort of man would go with her.' (page 58).

(iii) 'Sharon is a celebrity.' (page 59).

(iv) 'Sharon is suddenly wise.' (page 60).

(v) 'But Sharon is beyond them now. Beyond asking. Beyond telling.' (page 61).

d **By yourself**, write down your opinion on whether this story is mainly about Sharon's relationship with John, or about the other girls' reactions to it. Refer to the text to support your ideas.

Reading and response

e **As a class**, or **in groups**, consider three aspects of Valerie Thornton's story-telling technique by discussing the questions which follow:

How the story starts and ends

Re-read the first section of the story (from the beginning to '...life flowed around her') and the last section (from 'The next day she is pale and worried' to the end).

(i) In what ways does the first section portray Sharon as an 'outsider', cut off by circumstances from the other girls?

(ii) Compare the last section of the story with the first. Has the way in which we see Sharon changed? Could you say that, in a sense, the story has come full circle?

Episodes

The story of Sharon and John's relationship is presented by the writer in five distinct episodes. Look up the way in which each of these episodes begins: the first three start with exactly the same words, 'One day', the last two with a sentence including the phrase 'the next day'.

Why do you think Valerie Thornton chooses to tell the story in this 'episodic' way? Does it, in your opinion, make the story dull and repetitive, or does it add to its effectiveness? If so, why?

Tenses

Some parts of the story are told in the past tense ('Sharon walked alone'); some are written in the present tense ('She thinks a little, then shrugs her shoulders').

Find at least three points in the story where Valerie Thornton changes the tense from past to present and back again. Can you, as a reader, see any purpose in these tense changes? Would your response to the story have been the same if the writer has used only the past tense throughout?

f **By yourself**, choose a subtitle for this story which you feel sums up its main themes. Write an explanation of how it does so, referring to the text to illustrate the points you make.

7 Written activities linked to *Sharon, the Ferryman's Daughter*

By yourself, write on one or more of the following topics:

a Imagine that Sharon keeps a secret diary. Write four or five entries she makes in it during the time described in the story. The exact points you choose for the entries are up to you to decide.

What you write will depend partly on whether you think she is telling the whole truth. Make sure you describe Sharon's feelings about how the girls react to what she tells them.

b After Sharon stops coming to school altogether, the head teacher has to write an official report about her. Apart from the head's own knowledge of Sharon, she consults the following people to help compile the report:

- Sharon's form teacher or tutor.
- Sharon's father.
- Some of the girls Sharon knew.

Write the report as if you are the head teacher. Include in it all the information you think will be important if Sharon goes:

- to another school.
- into employment.
- into the care of Social Services.

c Write a real or imagined story about someone of Sharon's age who is, either by choice or circumstances, a loner. The person concerned can be either male or female, and it is entirely up to you to bring out the reasons why they are so solitary.

Tell the story from whichever point of view best suits the impact you want to make on the reader.

8 End-of-Unit written assignments

Write on one or more of the following titles. Refer closely to the stories to back up your ideas and comments.

Subject-matter and themes

a Both Nick and Sharon experience problems in their relationships with the opposite sex. Explain what these problems are and why they have them. In your opinion, which of the two handles their difficulties better? Why?

b 'Neither Nick nor Sharon are really in love: they both just think they are.' Do you agree? What would you say are the strongest influences on their feelings towards Fleur and John respectively?

Story-telling techniques

c In *Love Letters*, Nick tells his own story in his own words. In *Sharon, the Ferryman's Daughter*, the story is told in the third person.

How well suited to each story are these different ways of telling? Do you find one technique more effective than the other, or are they both successful in their own way?

d Compare the endings of *Love Letters* and *Sharon, the Ferryman's Daughter*. Give your own understanding of how each story's ending is designed to bring home to us its main theme(s). In your opinion, do the endings achieve this successfully, or do they leave you feeling let down?

General

e Which of these two stories have you enjoyed the most? Back up your opinion by commenting on such things as:

- how well the storylines held your interest.
- how true-to-life you found the characters in each story.
- how interested you were in the stories' themes.

You may also refer to any of the matters raised in the other four assignments on this page.

UNIT FOUR

MYSTERIES

Barney

Will Stanton

In *Barney*, the action takes place on an island and is described through a series of diary entries. But who is the mysterious Barney? What exactly is happening on the island? And why is the diary writer under threat without realising it?

Woman and Home

Robert Westall

In *Woman and Home*, a teenage boy plays truant for a day. He hides up in an old, rambling house which seems to be unlived in. When the boy finds himself unable to get out, he starts to think he may not be alone. Is he really trapped by the house, and if so, why?

1 Pre-reading activity on both stories

Speaking and listening *Monster or myth?*

In a group, read the information below about the so-called 'Loch Ness Monster'. Consider all the points with an open mind. On the basis of the evidence, come to a conclusion which explains the mystery of the monster to your satisfaction.

Sightings

- The Loch Ness Phenomena Investigation Bureau report that since 1934 there have been nearly 4,000 accepted sightings of the monster.
- Well over half the sightings have been made in the months of July and August. About 90 per cent of them occur between dawn and 9.30 am.
- Those who report seeing the monster include tourists, scientists, local residents, and professional people of all kinds.

Facts about the Loch

- Loch Ness is the largest lake in Britain. It measures twenty-two miles in length and averages about a mile in width. Submarine research shows that it is nearly a thousand feet deep.
- The salt-water Loch is at least 10,000 years old and probably much older.

The monster's appearance

- Half the sightings give a clear account of the monster's head and neck. The majority describe a reptilian type of head, modified to include a snout and a pair of horns. It is held in an arch shape at a height of about six feet above the water. This is quite unlike any known living species of fish, mammal or reptile.
- The majority of sightings refer to the monster's humps. These vary in number from three to nine. The overall visible body length is about thirty feet. The humps appear to be solid, shaped like a steep-gabled house. No known animal is capable of producing such a body shape.
- Most sightings describe the monster's colour simply as 'dark'. Those which are more specific consistently state that the colour is either battleship-grey or reddish-brown.

Movement

This is a selection of comments from people who claim to have seen the monster, describing the way, and the speed at which, the monster moves:

‘Cruising along at twenty to thirty miles per hour – motionless for ten minutes – swimming at a furious rate – loafing in the water – basking on the surface – terrific speed like a motor boat – slow moving, then suddenly dashed forward with incredible speed – kept pace with the monster at 25 mph in my car – have never seen anything travel on water so fast, it streaked across the Loch – speed about thirty-five miles per hour – racing through the water at terrific speed’

The ITN Monster Hunt

- In 1969, an expedition from ITN went to Loch Ness on a fourteen-day search for the monster. Public interest in it had been renewed when a team from Birmingham University made a sonar search of the loch and claimed that it could well contain a monster.
- The fifty members of the ITN expedition used sophisticated under-water devices and kept a round-the-clock camera watch on the whole Loch. TV cameras were strategically placed around its shore line.
- Sonar equipment was used to sweep Loch Ness. A sonar 'curtain' was stretched vertically beneath the water, and a second sonar carried out a horizontal scan. Not once did the scientists' display screens show even the briefest 'blip' to indicate something unusual stirring in the Loch.
- The project organiser concluded, 'If there's anything in there, I don't see how it could have escaped our sonar beams. For me, it's the end of a legend.' ITN's chief reporter on the expedition, Richard Lindley, said, 'I'm still willing to believe the available evidence that points to the monster's existence. In my view, Nessie remains more than a myth.'

Possible reasons for the reported sightings

Apart from mass hallucination, the most common explanations for the vast number of sightings of the monster are:

- People see waterlogged tree trunks, freak waves, shadows on the water, etc.
- The 'monster' is really a type of prehistoric plesiosaur that has adapted itself to the cold water conditions of the Loch since it was cut off from the sea about 7,000 years ago.
- The whole thing is a gigantic hoax: the stories of a monster are deliberately invented to attract tourists to the area.

Now read *Barney*

BARNEY

August 30th

We are alone on the island now, Barney and I. It was a bit sad to have to sack Taylor after all these years, but I had no choice. The childish pranks he played I could have forgiven, but when he actually tried to poison Barney out of pure wickedness, he was standing in the way of scientific progress. And that I cannot allow.

I can only believe his attempt to poison Barney was made while he was under the influence of alcohol, it was so clumsy. The poison container was overturned and a trail of powder led to Barney's dish. Taylor's defence was pathetic: he tried to deny it! Since there was no one else on the island, who, apart from him, could have done it?

September 2nd

I don't feel so bad about sacking Taylor now. I suppose this isolated life on the island must have become too much for him. That, and having to abandon the use of his precious guinea pigs. He insisted right to the end that they were better suited than Barney to my experiments. He was a hard worker but not very bright, poor Taylor.

Anyway, now that I am by myself with Barney, I have complete freedom to carry on my work without interruption. And now Taylor has gone, it's amazing how much happier Barney seems to be! I have given him the complete run of the place, and what fun it is to see how his newly awakened mental curiosity carries him about. After only two weeks of the glutamic acid treatments, he has become interested in my library, dragging the books from the shelves and going over them page by page. I am sure he knows that there is some knowledge to be got from them – if only he knew how!

September 8th

For the past two days, I have had to keep Barney under strict observation – and how he hates being confined! I am afraid that after my experiments are finished I shall have to do away with Barney altogether. Ridiculous as it may sound, there is always a slight risk that he may be able to pass on his intelligence to others of his kind. However small the chance might be, the risk is too great to ignore. Fortunately, there is in the basement a vault built with the idea of keeping vermin out. It will do equally well to keep Barney in – for as long as necessary.

September 9th

It seems that I spoke too soon. Barney escaped! This morning I let him out for a moment to frisk around before we began a new series of tests. After a quick look around the room, he returned to his cage, sprang up on the door handle, removed the key with his teeth, and before I could stop him he was out of the window! By the time I reached the yard, I saw that he had got on to the coping-stones around the top of the well. I arrived on the spot only in time to hear the key splash into the water far below.

I confess I am rather embarrassed by this. It is the only key. The door is locked. There are some valuable papers in separate compartments inside the vaults. Fortunately, although the well is over forty feet deep, there are only a few feet of water in the bottom, so getting the key back will not be too much of a problem. But I must admit that Barney has won the first round!

September 10th

I have had a rather upsetting experience. Once again, in a minor clash with Barney, I have come off second best. On this occasion, I will admit that he acted like a hero and may even have saved my life.

In order to help myself to get down into the well, I knotted a length of three-quarter inch rope at one-foot intervals to make a simple ladder. I reached the bottom easily enough, but after only a few minutes of groping for the key, my torch batteries ran out and I returned to the surface. A few feet from the top, I heard excited squeaks from Barney, and when I reached ground level I noticed that the rope was almost completely severed. It seems that it had rubbed against the edge of the stonework and Barney, seeing the danger I was in, was doing his best to warn me.

I have now replaced the worn section of rope. I have put new batteries into my torch, and I am now ready for the final descent down the well. I have taken these few minutes off to give myself a breather and to bring my diary up to date. Perhaps I should make myself a sandwich, as I may be down there longer than seems likely at the moment.

September 11th

Poor Barney is dead an soon I shell be the same. He was a wonderfull ratt and life without him is knot worth livving. If anybody reeds this, please do not disturb anything on the island but leeve it like it is as a shryne to Barney, espechilly the old well. Do not look for my body as I will throwe myself into the see. You mite bring a couple of young ratts an leeve them as a living memorial to Barney. Females – no males. I sprayned my wrist is why this is written so bad. This is my laste will. Do what I say an don't come back or disturb anything after you bring the young ratts like I said. Just females.

Goodby

WILL STANTON

2 Post-reading activity on *Barney*

Speaking and listening *Story into film*

a **In a group**, plan a 15-minute film version of this story. It may, if you wish, take the form of an animated cartoon.

The time limit for this activity is half-an-hour. Your task is to *plan* the film, rather than to produce a 'polished' version of it.

Use whatever method of planning seems best to you: story-boarding, for example. Alternatively, you could hold a 'shooting conference' in which group members take on different roles: producer, script consultant, camera director, film editor, etc.

As you plan, concentrate on bringing out the elements of strangeness and mystery in the story.

b Finish this activity by holding a **class discussion** in which different groups describe what they have planned and the methods used. Include in your discussion any problems you have met with in turning *Barney* from a short story into a film.

3 Text focus

Reading for understanding

a **In a group**, re-read the last diary entry, for 11 September. Discuss the following questions about it:

- Who has written it? How do you know?
- How is this possible?
- What does the last entry say has happened to the writer of the diary? Is this true?
- Why does the last entry include the two requests: 'please do not disturb anything on the island…bring a couple of young ratts…Females – no males'?
- Did you predict that the last entry in the diary would take this form? If so, what gave you the main clues?

b The writer of *Barney*, Will Stanton, creates a feeling of mystery partly by using 'red herrings' to mislead or puzzle the reader.

With a partner, examine the way he does this by looking back to the end of each of the first five diary entries. After each one, say what the writer wants us to think is happening and what is likely to happen next. For example, after the entry for 30 August:

- who or what did you think Barney was?
- why did the writer of the diary make such a big issue of Taylor?
- why did you think Taylor may have tried to poison Barney?

When you have finished, **join up with another pair**. Compare the red herrings you have identified. Have you reached similar conclusions about what their purpose is?

c **As a class**, discuss whether *Barney* raises any serious themes and issues, or whether Will Stanton's only purpose is to entertain and intrigue the reader. During your discussion, consider whether the story:

- says anything important about experimenting on live animals.
- warns human beings about thinking of themselves as controllers of the natural world.
- paints a disturbing picture of a possible future.

d **By yourself**, write an account of why, in your opinion, Will Stanton wrote this story and what effect he means it to have on the reader. Whatever you decide, say, with reasons, whether you think he succeeds in his aims.

Reading and response

e **As a class**, or **in groups**, consider three aspects of Will Stanton's story-telling technique by discussing the questions which follow:

Diary form

What purposes are served by telling the story in the form of diary entries that could not be served by writing it in other ways? In particular, does the diary form:

- create suspense?
- leave us to work out for ourselves what is going on?
- reveal more about the person writing the diary?

Personal narrative style

Since the whole story is composed of extracts from a diary, it has a very personal style and is written from a particular point of view. How does Will Stanton make use of this device to direct the reader's response?

(i) To begin your discussion, say what impressions of the diary writer's character are conveyed by the following entries and by the language and tone in which they are written:

- '...he was standing in the way of scientific progress. And that I cannot allow.' (entry 1)
- 'That, and having to abandon the use of his precious guinea pigs...He was a hard worker but not very bright, poor Taylor.' (entry 2)
- 'I am afraid that after my experiments are finished I shall have to do away with Barney altogether.' (entry 3)
- 'On this occasion, I will admit that he acted like a hero and may even have saved my life.' (entry 5)

(ii) Contrast the style and viewpoint of entries 1 to 5 with those of entry 6. What point may the writer be making through this contrast?

Sub-text

Responding in full to the meaning of a story often involves reading 'between the lines'. There may be more than one version of events, particularly in a personal narrative such as *Barney*.

(i) Consider this other version, or sub-text, by putting yourself in Barney's place. Say what account *he* might give of the events described in entries 2 to 5. For example, what might Barney's version be of:

- 'I am sure he knows that there is some knowledge to be got from them – if only he knew how!' (entry 2)
- '...Barney, seeing the danger I was in, was doing his best to warn me.' (entry 5)

(ii) How does Will Stanton's use of sub-text help to bring out the story's themes?

f **By yourself**, write an explanation of why Will Stanton has chosen the diary form as his way of telling this story. When planning your work, draw on the discussion you have had in **a** above.

4 Written activities linked to *Barney*

By yourself, write on one or more of the following topics:

a Imagine that Barney is able to read and write from the beginning of the story. Compose the five entries he makes in his personal diary for the period 30 August to 10 September inclusive.

You may describe any aspects of life on the island you wish, as well as Barney's private thoughts and feelings. It is likely that he would give his own reaction to the events mentioned by the scientist.

b Research and write about any one of the following subjects on which you have strong views:

- Vivisection.
- The use of live animals for scientific experiments.
- Conservation *or* man's interference with the world of nature.
- Hunting animals for sport.
- Vegetarianism *or* veganism.

Set out your writing in either of these ways:

(i) Compile a 'protest pamphlet' in which you draw the attention of adult readers to something you feel to be wrong. Set out and write the pamphlet in a way that will persuade others to share your point of view. Include illustrations, statistics, quotations, etc. If you wish, use a computer to produce your final version.

(ii) Devise a leaflet for younger readers who know little or nothing about your chosen topic. Your purpose is to inform and educate them about it. When planning, bear in mind the need for a suitable form of presentation and language level, so that these readers will understand the information. If you wish, use a computer to produce your final version.

c Write a story entitled *The Rat Revolution: Barney's Revenge*.

Assume that enough time has passed since the last diary entry for all of Barney's requests to be granted. The island rats are now ready to mount a full-scale attack against humans. Describe what happens. Write the story in any form you consider suitable.

Now read *Woman and Home*

WOMAN AND HOME

The house caught him, the first time he played truant from school. Playing truant wasn't a habit. This was the first time. The trouble was, he was new at the school, and not fitting in. He'd come from a county grammar, and this was a city comprehensive. He had a posh accent he wasn't able to hide. Anyway, why should he? It was his voice.

He was bullied; but he didn't bully easy. He was tall and thin, but quick and not soft. When Brewster tried twisting his arm, he gave Brewster a very bloody nose. That should have finished it, especially as Brewster was far from heroic in defeat. It *would* have finished it, at his old grammar school.

But this was a city comprehensive, and not a well-run one. Brewster went to his Head of Year to complain, and it was the victim who got the telling-off.

'We don't hold with physical violence in this school,' said the Head. 'We find talking things out peacefully is better.'

He shook hands with Brewster in front of the Head. But afterwards Brewster was not inclined to talk things out peacefully; he summoned his gang. It never came to fists again. No, it was endless little things that weren't worth reporting. Like being tripped up in the corridor; or having your bag snatched from under your arm, and tipped out under the feet of the trampling herd. Or having 'London Pouf' scrawled on your locker-door with lipstick, or having your trousers dumped under the shower if you weren't back first from games.

They never seemed to tire of it. And after a month came the morning he just couldn't face any more of it. He turned away back towards the city centre.

He solved one problem, and immediately a lot of others landed on his head. Had any of his class seen him duck down the side-street? They would certainly report *him* to the form-master.

And here was one of them coming towards him up the side-street now...

He ducked away like a rabbit, into an even more ramshackle side-street, lined with rusty corrugated sheds in a sea of rose-bay willowherb, and realised the city centre wasn't for him today. It would be full of teachers nipping out to do a bit of shopping in their free period, governors who would recognise his uniform, his mum's new friends and neighbours...

So he wandered the back-streets; until it started to rain. Pretty heavily. Where on earth could he *go*? Mum only worked part time, and she would be home all day, doing the washing and ironing. They knew him at the library, the bowling-alley was shut; there was no cinema matineé till two o'clock, and *they'd* just ring school anyway.

The only place in the world was a derelict shed with the door hanging off its hinges. He slipped in like a thief. The floor was wet mud, a pattern of footprints filling with water from a big puddle in the middle. There were two big blue oil-drums lying on their sides, and a heap of black and white ash, where somebody had tried setting fire to the end wall. Somebody else had scrawled, in huge letters of yellow chalk, BANANA-LEGS IS A BUMMER.

Banana-legs was what they called the Head, because he braced his legs back tensely while waiting for something like silence to fall in assembly.

The evil-doers had been here before him; this was where *they* came when they were playing truant and it rained.

He was one of them now. He was sure some kid would have reported him. The Head would ring his mum. Trouble with Dad who was already worried sick about his new job...

He wished he was back in school. School might be hell, but it was better than *this*. He looked at his watch; an age seemed to have passed; but it was only twenty past nine. Soon, they'd be coming out of assembly. If he ran, could he slip in with them to first lesson?

But he knew even if he ran like mad he'd never make it. He'd arrive wet and sweating in the middle of the lesson, to face questions and jeers.

The rain fell heavier, making a noise like machine-guns on the tin roof. What could he *do*?

First lesson was English. In a desperate attempt to be a law-abiding citizen, he got out his English book, sat on a blue oil-drum and tried to read. But it was too dark. And drops of water from the leaking roof began falling on his head.

The quality of the light changed. He looked up, to see a cat peering in the door. A cheerful-looking black cat, with a white bib. It seemed a godsend...he was good at making friends with cats. He held out his hand, called gently to it.

It gave him a look of sheer contempt and vanished.

Even the cat didn't want him...

He packed up his books in a frenzy; as he did so, his English exercise-book fell into the mud. Open. At the English essay he'd spent two hours on last night. A *good* essay, because he *liked* English.

He fastened his bag and ran out of that dreadful place like a mad thing; just wanting to get away. Anywhere.

That was when the house caught him.

It was the sun shining on the wet back of his neck that brought him to his senses. He looked around in surprise. It had stopped raining; the sky was blue, with only a few little friendly fluffy clouds. And he was utterly lost. But still he was afraid somebody might drive past in a car and see him. They said the Heads of Year spent half their days driving round the town looking for truants out of school. He *must* get under cover.

There was a high, overgrown privet hedge. A giant, obscene privet hedge like a young forest, ten feet high. And a double white gate. Half the gate was open. It drooped into the gravel as if it hadn't been moved in years. The paint was peeling off, leaving the wood beneath dark and soggy. Beyond, a worn gravel drive wound round to the left. There were tall thin fronds of grass growing out of the drive, all over. Dry and dead, last year's grass. Nobody must have gone up that drive for ages. It was *inviting*. Well, at least the passing cars wouldn't see him...

Even Brewster might've warned him. But Brewster wasn't there.

It was a funny garden. He helped Dad with the garden at home, so he soon spotted just how funny it was. Nobody had touched it for years; but it was OK. It hadn't turned into a jungle. He could see where weeds had tried to grow; but the weeds had died. They lay like shrivelled little pale corpses though it was high summer. Whereas the garden plants and flowers were doing fine. Mind you, they needed pruning; the roses had put out branches ten feet high, that waved in the warm breeze like crazy fishing-rods. But they were doing OK.

Perhaps that should've warned him, too. But he passed up the formal garden, suddenly happy and peaceful and feeling at home. Up the stone steps, between the mossy pair of urns, up to the statue and the lily pond, where the white flowers were just breaking the surface, and the goldfish big as herring swam in the green depths. He wondered what the goldfish fed on...

He looked up, and saw the house.

He had to squint at it, because the sun was above it, and the sun was also reflecting up from the dark water of the lily pond.

He couldn't make out if anyone was at home or not. There was no smoke coming from the white chimneys, but then it was summer.

There were no broken windows, or slates off the roof. There were curtains at the windows, and stuff inside.

On the other hand, there was a white verandah with wistaria growing up the pillars. Lumps of the wistaria had grown out uncontrolled, and been tugged free of their wires by the wind, and hung in great loose clumps, swaying, as nobody who loved plants would've allowed. Nobody in their right mind would've allowed. They swayed crazily, dangerously.

The other odd thing was the half bricks lying on the paths between him and the house. Not many, but placed temptingly. Tempting you to hurl them into the lily pond, or through the glass of the frail conservatory.

The temptation *annoyed* him; because he was not that sort of person. It wasn't that he was a goody-goody, or teacher's pet. It was because he *liked* lily ponds and conservatories and old houses...So he carefully picked the half-bricks from the paths, and tucked them away out of sight, before they tempted somebody else.

In the same way, when he reached the verandah, he couldn't help fastening back the wistaria inside its wires as best he could, and neatly pruning off the rest with his pocket-knife. It seemed to *want* to be done, somehow...

And then a door banged, round the corner of the verandah. He stood, paralysed with the knowledge that somebody lived here after all; blushing from head to foot with embarrassment that they must have been watching him, fiddling with their wistaria. Such enormous *cheek*...he waited, wild-eyed, trembling.

But the minutes passed, and nobody came. In the end, he moved, his legs stiff with tension. Round the corner…

There was a door. A double door, with glass panes in the top. One half was open. But as he watched, it swung closed in the wind, with the same bang. Then, in the next gust of wind, it swung open again.

And closed.

Then open again. The paint on the door was peeling off in great curls, like the paint on the gate. As the door slammed open and shut, great flakes fell off, to join flakes already lying on the verandah. It said quite clearly to him that nobody had lived there for ages. But if it was allowed to go on slamming in the wind, sooner or later the glass would break, the door would come off its hinges, the rain would get in.

He walked forward to shut the door safely.

And saw the huge heap of letters lying on the doormat inside. Like they'd found at home, when they came back from a fortnight's holiday. He peered down at them. The ones at the bottom were browning with age and rain and mingled with brown leaves that had blown in, but the ones on top looked quite new. Again, it offended him; it was a breach in the sensible world. He leaned through, and gathered them up, crouching on his heels and swaying dangerously, for he had a reluctance to put a foot inside. Then he retired to the fence of the verandah and sorted them into order by postmark. The oldest were over a year old, but some were only a week. Most of it was junk, addressed to the 'The Occupier' but there was one addressed to 'Miss Nadine Marriner' in a small, mean, spidery hand. And somehow the name made him shudder, in spite of the warmth of the sun on his back. Miss Nadine Marriner – it had a thin spiteful sound, he thought.

There were a couple of elastic bands round some of the letters. He used them to make the whole thing into a neat bundle. But what to do with the bundle? He looked through the glass panes and saw a hall table, and a grandfather clock.

Well then, put them all on the hall table, slam the door shut properly, so it wouldn't blow open again, and that was *that*. Somehow, although he liked the garden a lot, he didn't like the house so much. It looked dark inside, after the sunny garden.

He stepped in, and put the letters on the table. Looked at the grandfather clock. He sometimes went round the antique fairs with Dad. Dad liked to buy up old stopped clocks cheap, mend them, and sell them at a profit. Notes in your hand and not a word to the Inland Revenue.

This clock was stopped. But he could also see it was a very good one, with a silvered brass face, and brass tops to the columns, and a little brass eagle on top. Even with the dead leaves gathered in a drift round its base, it looked what Dad called a two-thousand-pound clock…He opened the door in the base, and looked inside. The pendulum was properly hung, the weights in place, but run down right to the floor. That was why the clock had stopped. He reached automatically for the shelf where keys were usually kept. The key was there. Unthinking, he put it into the winding-holes, and wound up the heavy weights and swung the pendulum.

Immediately the clock began to tick, a slow stately beat, that was a comfort to the ear. It seemed gently to bring the whole house alive.

Then suddenly, without warning, it chimed. Loud and long, it struck ten, though the hands pointed to half past two. He knew he shouldn't be alarmed. When clocks wound down, the chime sometimes got out of synch, as Dad said. But the chimes were so *loud* and triumphant; as if the clock was telling the whole house, the whole world, that he had come. He suddenly felt he had done something irrevocable. He turned to run...

He heard the door slam shut in the wind, behind him.

Oh, well, open, shut, open, shut.

But when he pulled at the brass handle, green with lack of polishing, he found the lock had really worked this time. The door was really shut. And, what's more, struggle as he might, he couldn't get it open again.

Well, he told himself bravely, there will be other doors; or windows at a pinch, if they weren't painted up solid. He moved forward into the house, among the shadows. Outside, the sun had gone in...

He had a funny desire, every few paces, to stop and listen for other footsteps. Especially footsteps upstairs. That locked door made a difference. Before, one sound and he could have taken to his heels, and been out of the house and out of the garden in less than a minute. Now he was...

A prisoner. No longer free. If somebody came, he would have to do what they said...

The sooner he got out of here, the better.

He went into the first room with an open door. It seemed less cheeky. Less dangerous than trying one of the closed doors.

This was obviously the kitchen. Huge cold black kitchen range, and a battered electric cooker that must have been 1950s. Stone-flagged floor, with beetles scurrying away into the dark corners. The sink was full of dirty dishes, on to which the cold tap dripped, its sound quarrelling with the ticking of the clock that had followed him in. Every work-surface was covered with an intricate clutter, like a spider's web to catch the eye. He got a feel of Miss Nadine Marriner's mind, somehow. A muddled, devious, cluttered mind. He didn't like it. His mum kept their kitchen spotlessly tidy.

But the huge pine table in the middle of the kitchen held different kinds of things. A packet of cigarettes, with one taken out, smoked, and left as a trampled-out stub on the floor. A tin, with three crude rough-looking cigarettes inside, that smelt funny when he sniffed them. Reefers?

A bottle of whisky, half-empty. And a glass with a thin damp brown stain on the bottom.

He sniffed without touching. Yes, it was whisky all right.

Again, he was tempted. But he'd tried whisky, and hated the taste. And his first and only cigarette had made him sick. Besides, he didn't know where they'd been.

He left them alone.

He looked under the table. There was a huge dirty bundle there; a sleeping-bag wrapped round what looked like trousers and sweaters, with an enamel mug attached by a length of coarse white string.

A tramp's bundle. A man-tramp, from the smell of it.

So now he had a tramp to worry about as well. An old lady was one thing. But a tramp who probably stole whisky and reefers was a lot more scary.

C'mon, let's get out of here. Quick. He moved swiftly to the kitchen door. Undid the bolts, top and bottom. But it was locked as well, with a huge old fashioned lock. And the key wasn't in it. He searched the cluttered work-surface in vain, feeling he was wasting time he could ill afford.

Well, other rooms then. With a verandah, there were bound to be french windows.

The next room did have french windows.

And a dog lying down next to them, asleep. Probably the tramp's dog. If he tried to get out through the french windows it might wake up and bark, or even attack him. The tramp would come. From upstairs. He kept having this funny feeling there was somebody upstairs.

He studied the dog carefully. It didn't look dangerous. It was a small brown mongrel, with floppy ears. Oh, he could deal with that. He tiptoed forwards, trying not to wake it. Reached the french windows, and twisted the handle.

It didn't open. He saw with despair the empty keyhole. Almost felt the dog reaching to bite his ankle. It must have heard, must have awakened.

But it still lay there. It lay there, still. *Too* still. Its belly wasn't going up and down. It wasn't *breathing*.

It must be *dead*. He looked down at it in horror. It still looked just...asleep. Comfortably asleep. There was no smell or maggots or any kind of nastiness, like fur falling off. Not like the dogs you saw floating drowned in the river...

He *had* to touch it. He didn't want to, but he *had* to.

It moved dryly, all of a piece, like a statue.

It was a stuffed dog. A real dog, real skin and fur, that had died and been stuffed. Nothing to do with any tramp. This had cost a lot of money. It must have been Miss Nadine Marriner's pet, that had died. She must have had it stuffed and gone on living with it.

What a crazy thing to do, living with a dead stuffed pet!

Then he wished he hadn't thought that. It wasn't nice to think Miss Nadine Marriner was crazy. But it explained the open door, and the leaves blowing in on priceless antiques, and the pile of unopened letters. He listened. Listened especially for ceilings creaking, which would mean somebody moving, upstairs. But there was just silence, and the ticking of the clock.

He looked longingly outside, through the glass of the french windows. There, at the end of the garden, was the drooping white gate. Beyond, cars would be passing. Far off, his class would be having their break. He could break the glass, get out that way. The sun was shining out there again.

But it wouldn't mean just breaking one pane of glass. It would mean breaking the french windows.

And he couldn't do that.

Well, there were plenty more rooms, Get on with it. You're just being silly. This is Monday morning the 3rd of October 1988, and Mum is at home doing the washing. What could possibly happen?

As he turned to go back to the door, he saw the rocking chair. A big American rocker with a green upholstered back and seat. The upholstery was old, worn and greasy. And it seemed to bear the marks of a thin body, worn into it with time. There was a hooky mat beneath it, worn through to the canvas where two feet had pressed. There was a bag hanging on one arm of the chair, a cracked plastic bag, with a trail of tangled grey knitting dangling from it. On the other side of the chair, on the dusty carpet, was a cup and saucer, with a dry brown stain on the bottom.

He just knew this was where Miss Nadine Marriner had sat all day, knitting something the dullest grey colour imaginable. She was so much *there* that he gave a little humble apologetic bob of his head, and said absurdly, 'I'm sorry. I'm just going. When I can find a way out.'

The moment he spoke, he knew it was a mistake. Speaking to the chair made Miss Nadine Marriner more real in his mind. He could imagine her, now. Very thin, with gold-rimmed spectacles and grey hair pulled back in a bun, and knobbled veined thin hands, knitting, knitting. He couldn't *move*, for looking at the chair. He couldn't make his legs work, standing facing the empty chair, with the stuffed dog at his back.

Then with a yell like a feeble war-cry, he moved and leapt past the chair. As he passed it, he must have caught it with his sleeve. For when he glanced back from the doorway, it was rocking, rocking.

Frantic, now, he tried other doors. All were locked. And he could tell from trying to force the handles that they were very solid Victorian doors. And from under one came the foulest smell he had ever smelt. A smell of utter rottenness. Like the time they came back from holiday, and the freezer had broken down, and the smell of that joint of pork Mum had been keeping for their return...

But he consoled himself that that door was plain, and next to the kitchen. Must be the pantry door. Some meat must have been left, and gone rotten inside. He thought he heard the buzz of a bluebottle, through the thick woodwork.

But he could've been imagining it. He knew he was in a very odd mood, one he'd never been in before. His body was shaky, his mind all whirly. He was starting to be silly and imagine things. He must get a grip on himself.

He must go upstairs. Look for keys, he told himself. So he wouldn't have to start smashing his way out...But he knew he was kidding himself.

Upstairs was calling him. He didn't want to go up there; he didn't want the shock of opening any more doors, of walking into rooms where he didn't know what he might see. The tramp asleep, snoring. Suddenly opening his eyes. Or Miss Nadine Marriner, standing watching him. Or Miss Nadine Marriner dead in her bed.

He hovered piteously in the hall, looking out through the glass in the door at the sunlit garden. Again, he contemplated smashing the glass, knocking out every sharp edge and crawling through to freedom. But suppose somebody came, while he was doing it…

Finally, he turned, and slowly began to climb the stairs. The stair-carpet was thick, but old and grey and full of dust. The dust shot up in clouds from his feet. Hung golden in the shafts of sunlight streaming down from the window on the landing above. The dust of Miss Nadine Marriner, creeping, sweet and sour, into his body through his nostrils, so he wanted to stop breathing.

And the sun was shining down the stairs so brightly, he couldn't see if there was anybody standing at the top of the stairs, waiting for him.

But there wasn't. There was just the window. It was clear in the middle (though very much spattered by dirty rain) but blue and red stained-glass round the edges. Through it, he could see what appeared to be the kitchen garden. Again, not much in the way of weeds, but cabbages sprouting to a great height with yellow strings of flowers. And beyond the garden, quite far off, a kind of summer-house with glass windows.

And the window in the door was broken.

And through the jagged hole, he could see what looked like a flat bloated figure, half lying, half sitting inside. He might have thought it was a bundle of dark old clothes, except he could see the head, and a blurred sort of face, with dark holes for eyes, looking up at him in a rather pleading way. It gave him quite a turn, though it must have been fifty or sixty feet away, just sitting there, staring up at this window.

Then he realised it must be a made-up stuffed figure, a Guy Fawkes or a scarecrow, because the face was all weird colours, green and purple, and the eyes were just holes.

He had enough worries, without scarecrows stored in summer-houses. Find a key, and get out!

The first three doors were locked. Again he smelt, more faintly, the smell of rotting pork; but he thought it must be drifting upstairs from the larder. For it was *very* much fainter.

The last door was half open. But the room beyond was dim, as if the curtains were drawn. He hovered, listening. No sound at all; except the ticking of the clock, coming up the stairs behind. He sniffed. There was a very strong smell of old lady. Lavender and powder, old sweat and the sickly sweetness of age. He felt pulled forwards, as the receding waves had tried to suck him out to sea last summer. But he fought against it, now. As if he knew once he was sucked into that room, he would never come out again.

And then, downstairs, the clock struck eleven. The clang seemed to fill the whole house. And it was as if it was announcing his presence outside that door.

He was caught. He had to walk in.

There was a figure standing straight opposite him, in the gloom of the drawn curtains. A figure that watched him with eyes that glared out of a white face, standing stock-still.

It was no bigger than he himself. It made no move to attack, standing with its arms by its sides. It looked…

Hopeless, helpless, drowned in the green gloom.

He half raised an arm, to ward off the terrified glare.

The figure in turn raised its arm.

And then he saw it was himself; caught in the long mirror of a wardrobe. But lost, drowned, frozen as if under green ice.

He tried to force a laugh; it failed, making a weird mad sound in that dim silent room. But it released him to move.

He swung round to look behind the door, where the bed would be…

The bed was made, pulled flat and tight. Nothing to be afraid of there. He looked under the bed; nothing but the dim shine of a white chamber pot. He let his eyes pan to the left. A chair with a heap of old lady's dark clothes piled up on it. Another mirror, above a dressing-table, as cluttered as the kitchen work-surfaces downstairs. Miss Nadine Marriner's, without a doubt. Then a tall dark chest of drawers, with half the drawers pulled open, and pale female things hanging out.

Then the big white marble fireplace, and above it…

Miss Nadine Marriner stared down at him.

Larger than life. Seated in the rocking-chair from down-stairs, with her knobbled veined hands clutching the wooden arms with a grip that said 'Mine, mine, *mine*!' she looked exactly as he had imagined her, when he first saw the rocking-chair. Tall, very bony, with gold-rimmed spectacles and her grey hair pulled back tight in a bun.

A portrait. A picture in oils, in a huge gilt frame. Just a huge oil-painting. But how could he have known so exactly what she would look like, before he saw the portrait?

And why did the face stare at him so, the eyes seeming to burn right through him, as if she was alive? Why did it make him feel so small, so helpless, so…obedient? Why did her presence seem to fill the whole room, the whole house? And why did he stand so submissive, waiting for her to…

Speak. He was waiting for her to speak; to give him orders. To obey her every whim, even as he saw, without hope, the cruelty in her, the lack of any sort of kindness or mercy.

He waited.

And then he saw the picture was a little crooked; it sloped down a little to the right.

He must set it straight. Slowly he walked up to it, closer and closer to those claw hands, those piercing eyes.

He tried to straighten the picture by grasping the two bottom corners. But the picture wouldn't move; it seemed stuck to the wall. He tried to pull it away, towards him.

As it moved and straightened, something fell down from behind it, bounced on the marble top of the mantelpiece, and fell among the soot-splashes that the rain had left on the green tiles of the hearth.

A thick brown letter.

Well, he couldn't just leave it there, getting dirty among the soot. He picked it up, and read the writing on the envelope.

TO THE FINDER.

That was *him*. And he was in no state to disobey the tall, spiky, spidery handwriting of Miss Nadine Marriner.

Inside was another envelope, and a note.

The note said, DELIVER THIS BY HAND TO THE ADDRESS ON THE ENVELOPE.

The envelope was addressed to a firm of solicitors in the city centre. It was open, and he could not help being curious. He looked up at the piercing eyes of Miss Nadine Marriner, and strangely they did not forbid him.

He opened the envelope, and unfolded the large stiff piece of paper. It was headed, THE LAST WILL AND TESTAMENT OF NADINE MARRINER, DECEASED.

He shuddered a little, and read on.

> I AM DEAD. HAVE NO DOUBT ABOUT THAT. DO NOT LOOK FOR MY CORPSE. YOU WILL NEVER FIND IT. I AM IN A VERY SAFE PLACE.
>
> BUT I LEAVE MY HOUSE, LANDS, AND ALL I AM POSSESSED OF TO THE BEARER OF THIS LETTER. I HAVE FOUND HIM HONEST AND TRUSTWORTHY. HE WILL CARE FOR THE HOUSE AND MY POSSESSIONS NOW I AM DEAD. HE GETS IT ONLY ON CONDITION THAT HE SELLS NOTHING, BUT LIVES IN THIS HOUSE, AND KEEPS IT AS IT IS AND IN GOOD REPAIR AS LONG AS HE SHALL LIVE.
>
> AS FOR THE OTHERS WHO CAME, THE THIEVES WHO TRIED TO STEAL, THE VANDALS WHO CAME TO SMASH AND BURN, FIND THEM WHERE YOU MAY AND BURY THEM WHERE YOU WILL. THEY BROUGHT THEIR DEATH UPON THEMSELVES.

There was more, and signatures at the bottom. Miss Nadine Marriner and two others he couldn't read.

The phrases hammered through his head. 'They brought their death upon themselves...Find them where you may and bury them where you will.'

He remembered the bloated green-faced scarecrow who had glared up at him so pleadingly from the broken glass of the summer-house. The awful smell in the room downstairs...The whole house was a *trap*. He remembered the half-bricks he had been tempted to throw in the lily pond, and at the frail conservatory. The whisky and the cigarettes and the reefers on the kitchen table. How many more traps?

And he knew she *was* still here. In the house. He had a weird feeling she was behind that tomb-like marble fireplace, still sitting upright in her chair, her hands clutched on the arms, saying 'Mine, mine, *mine*.' The whole house was full of her. It was as if she had moved out of her tall frail body, into the bricks and mortar, the glass and wood, the very soil itself, poisoning the intruding weeds...What had the huge goldfish fed on, to stay alive all this time?

There was no way out. He was trapped, finished. He must obey her, or he would never get out of here. And if he obeyed her, he would be caught up with her in a bargain, till the day he died...

And then he remembered the pile of letters on the doormat. The postman must have walked up the path nearly every day, and walked out again untouched.

Because he was innocent. Because he was just delivering letters, whistling to himself, thinking about something else.

It gave him a bit of courage. Enough to put everything back in the big envelope, and to say firmly, 'No thanks,' and to lift the portrait and tuck the letter back where it had come from.

He was frightened it might fall out again; with a dreadful insistence; as a dreadful warning.

But it stayed where it was. So he went while the going was good. Down the dust-laden stairs, to the front door. Through its glass he could see his schoolbag lying on the verandah, where he'd left it, what seemed like half a lifetime ago.

He put his hand on the dark-green brass of the door handle and tried it.

It turned first time, and he grabbed his bag and was off the verandah, tearing past the goldfish pond, down the steps between the urns, and out through the white gate.

He was still running when he heard a voice bellow.

'*HIGGINSON*!'

He stopped because that was his name. He had a feeling that the voice had been bellowing it for some time.

He was in the city centre, between the McDonald's and the video shop. He had no idea what streets he had run down. What streets he must have crossed, though he had a vague memory of car-horns hooting.

'Higginson? Where the hell do you think you are going? What's got into you, lad?'

It was Toddser Todd, Head of Third Year, glaring at him through the wound-down window of his Ford Fiesta, his red face clashing horribly with his ginger hair.

He didn't like Toddser much; didn't trust him. But at that moment, he felt like flinging his arms around his neck. But he only went over, and leaned against the car's bonnet, shaking all over.

'Get in,' said Toddser. 'You're in trouble, real trouble. This will have to go to the Head. You kids think you can get away with murder...'

He got in, and held his bag tight on his knee, so that Toddser wouldn't see how much his legs were shaking. But Toddser wasn't interested. He was still cruising the town centre, peering down every street they came to, looking for other truants, and at the same time mumbling the same old crap about order and discipline that he must mumble to all the kids he caught. But you could tell he was pleased to have caught somebody; you could tell he enjoyed the game.

'You're in *real* trouble,' went on Toddser like a tape-recording. 'You don't know what real trouble is like, till now...'

'I won't do it again, sir,' he said, with a great deal of fervour. So that Toddser, halted at a traffic-light, stared at him as if he was seeing him for the first time and said,

'You sound as if you really mean it.'

Then the lights changed, and Toddser drove back to school, and he closed his eyes and relaxed into the paradise of the real trouble to come. Knowing he could never find that white gate again. Even if he *tried*.

ROBERT WESTALL

5 Post-reading activity on *Woman and Home*

Speaking and listening *Flow-charting the story*

a **With a partner**, read the five quotations below which suggest that Higginson is somehow being summoned or 'called' by Miss Nadine Marriner into her presence:

- 'That was when the house caught him.' (page 78)
- 'It was *inviting*.' (page 79)
- 'A prisoner. No longer free.' (page 81)
- 'He must go upstairs.' (page 83)
- 'He was caught. He had to walk in.' (page 84)

Working together, trace Higginson's progress from the moment he enters the house to the point at which he comes face to face with Miss Marriner's portrait.

b Begin by making a series of brief notes. For example:

- *Verandah door slams shut (page 81).*
- *Front door locks by itself: won't open, no keys (page 81).*
- *Trapped in kitchen: bolts slide open but door locked (page 82).*

c Next, using a large sheet of paper, turn your completed notes into a flow chart. As well as illustrating Higginson's step-by-step progress towards Miss Marriner, your chart should show his failed attempts to escape. The final layout and design of your flow chart is up to you to decide. All that matters is that it should be accurate, clear and complete.

d Finish this activity by **joining up with another pair**. Compare your charts and explain why you have drawn yours as you have. Make any additions or alterations you consider necessary.

e How far does your flow chart suggest that Higginson is at the mercy of forces outside himself?

6 Text focus

Reading for understanding

a **In a group**, discuss the way in which, as you read the story, the feeling grows that Higginson is not in control of his own actions. Do this by imagining your group making a video version of *Woman and Home*. Select five key points from the story where the video would show Higginson being made against his will to move nearer and nearer to Miss Marriner. Say how you would bring this out in the video.

b **With a partner**, identify all the points in the story where Higginson could, in theory, have got out of the house. Briefly note down the reasons why, in each case, he does not escape.

c **As a class**, discuss the reasons why Higginson is eventually 'rewarded' by Miss Marriner with the gift of her house. How does this highlight a central theme in the story?

Reading and response

d **As a class**, or **in groups**, consider two aspects of Robert Westall's story-telling technique by discussing the questions which follow:

How the story starts and ends

(i) Re-read the first section of the story, from the start to 'That was when the house caught him.' (page 78) and the last section, from 'He was still running when he heard a voice bellow. "*HIGGINSON!*"' (page 87) to the end.

(ii) What impressions of Higginson's character are given in the opening section? What indications are there, if any, that this is going to be a story of mystery and the supernatural? Why might Robert Westall have chosen to begin *Woman and Home* in this way?

(iii) Do you feel that the ending is effective in rounding off the story? Would it have made any difference to your response if the story had ended with Higginson running wildly out of the house, '...tearing past the goldfish pond, down the steps between the urns, and out through the white gate.' (page 87)?

Setting and atmosphere

The setting for almost the whole story is Miss Marriner's house.

(i) Consider the atmosphere which the following extracts create, both on their own and cumulatively:

- 'Lumps of wistaria had grown out uncontrolled...They swayed crazily, dangerously.' (page 79).
- 'Immediately the clock began to tick...Then suddenly, without warning, it chimed. Loud and long, it struck ten, though the hands pointed to half past two.' (page 81).
- 'There was a huge dirty bundle there; a sleeping-bag wrapped round what looked like trousers and sweaters, with an enamel mug attached by a length of coarse white string.' (pages 81–82).
- 'It lay there, still. *Too* still. Its belly wasn't going up and down. It wasn't *breathing*.' (page 82).
- 'A big American rocker with a green upholstered back and seat...As he passed it, he must have caught it with his sleeve. For when he glanced back from the doorway, it was rocking, rocking.' (page 83).
- 'And through the jagged hole, he could see what looked like a flat bloated figure...he could see the head, and a blurred sort of face, with dark holes for eyes...' (page 84).
- 'He sniffed. There was a very strong smell of old lady. Lavender and powder, old sweat and the sickly sweetness of age.' (page 84).
- 'What had the huge goldfish fed on, to stay alive all this time?' (page 87).

(ii) Find further examples of descriptions which create a similar mood and atmosphere. What is their purpose? Do they merely create a vague feeling of menace and mystery? Or do they, for example, help explain why Higginson rejects Miss Marriner's gift to him of her home ('No thanks')?

End your discussion of these details of the setting by considering how they link in with Robert Westall's themes.

e **By yourself**, write a personal response to this story on the following title:

'*Woman and Home* is a mystery story with a moral. The sense of mystery and the supernatural is built up gradually and with great skill, but the writer does more than make us shiver. Through fear, Higginson learns some important truths about life.' Show how far you agree with this statement.

7 Written activities linked to *Woman and Home*

By yourself, write on one or more of the following topics:

a Re-read the whole of Miss Marriner's Last Will and Testament. Then tell the story of one or more of 'the others who came' to her house.

The form and viewpoint of the story are up to you to decide. In the light of the subject, your main purpose will be to build up a convincing atmosphere of mystery and/or horror.

b In *Woman and Home*, the writer concerns himself with thieving, vandalism and the destruction of property.

Imagine you are a reporter on your local newspaper. Write a front-page story about a burglary, an act of vandalism, or another crime against property that happens in your district.

Set out the story in an appropriate way and write in a suitable journalistic style. If you wish, use a computer to produce the final version of your front page.

c 'He was still cruising the town centre, peering down every street they came to, looking for other truants…'

Imagine that the problem of truancy among members of your year-group has recently increased. Your Head of Year has decided to write a letter to the parents or guardians of all pupils, in which he or she:

- outlines the nature and extent of the truancy problem.
- reminds parents of the penalties for truancy, and describes new sanctions which the school is about to introduce in an effort to reduce it.
- appeals for parents' help in stamping out the problem altogether.

Write the Head of Year's letter. Bear in mind that it is an official school document which will be written in a formal style.

8 End-of-Unit written assignments

Write on one or more of the following titles. Refer closely to the stories to back up your ideas and comments.

Subject-matter and themes

a In your opinion, which of these stories conveys the more serious and important message about the modern world? Give careful reasons for your view and refer to both stories in presenting it.

b Both the 'scientist' in *Barney* and Miss Marriner in *Woman and Home* are presented to us without any direct comment from the writers. As we read, we have to work out for ourselves what to make of them.

Describe the impressions you have formed of each character.

Story-telling techniques

c The setting for *Barney* is a remote island; the main setting for *Woman and Home* is a ramshackle house.

Compare the way in which Will Stanton and Robert Westall use these settings to build up an atmosphere of mystery and fear. In your opinion, which writer is the more successful in doing so? Why?

d Imagine that *Woman and Home* had been told by Higginson in diary form and that Barney had been told by Will Stanton as a third-person narrative. Do you think these alternative ways of telling would have made any difference to the effectiveness of the stories?

General

e *Barney* and *Woman and Home* are both mystery stories, but they are told in very different ways. Which of them do you consider is the more interesting and successful in creating a feeling of mystery? Which story do you think would make the better film?

UNIT FIVE

MARRIAGES

Telling Stories

Maeve Binchy

The two main characters in *Telling Stories* are about to get married. All the preparations have been made for their 'big day'. However, an unexpected event on the evening before the wedding leads to a slight change of plan.

One Wednesday Afternoon

Stan Barstow

The married couple in *One Wednesday Afternoon* have reached a point where their relationship is under some strain. A near-fatal accident forces them to examine the reasons why their marriage is not working.

1 Pre-reading activity on both stories

Speaking and listening *Commitments*

In a group, read the material that follows.

Some facts about marriage

A 1995 government publication, '*Marriage and Divorce Statistics*', revealed that:

- the number of people getting married is at its lowest level for 50 years.
- for every two weddings in England and Wales, one marriage ends in divorce.
- people are now marrying later – the average age for men is 28.2 years old and the average age for women is 26.2.

The traditional marriage service

The form of service still chosen by most couples who marry in church comes from *The Book of Common Prayer*, written in 1549. Here are the vows which each partner makes to the other:

I, __________ , take thee, __________ , to my wedded wife, to have and to hold from this day forward, for better for worse, for richer for poorer, in sickness and in health, to love and to cherish, till death us do part, according to God's holy ordinance; and thereto I give thee my troth.

I, __________ , take thee, __________ , to my wedded husband, to have and to hold from this day forward, for better for worse, for richer for poorer, in sickness and in health, to love, cherish, and to obey, till death us do part, according to God's holy ordinance; and thereto I give thee my troth.

The man, holding the ring, shall say:

With this ring, I thee wed, with my body I thee worship, and with all my worldly goods I thee endow; in the name of the Father, and of the Son, and of the Holy Ghost. Amen.

Alternative forms of commitment

In recent years it has become quite common for marrying couples to devise their own 'commitment' or 'contract' as an alternative to the traditional marriage service. These are two examples.

Alternative 1

I take you as my husband/wife because I love you and want to share everything in my life with you.

I promise to be loyal and faithful to you, as long as our love shall last. I pledge to share with you all I have, unless or until our two paths separate for reasons as yet unknown. I hope to be the father/mother of your children and vow to do my best to love, care and provide for them under whatever circumstances may arise in the future.

I intend not to hurt, abuse or take you for granted as we live out our lives together. I accept you joyfully as my married partner, hoping with all my heart to continue loving you as much as now I do.

Alternative 2

I love and want you; take me into your heart. I believe you love and want me; receive me into your soul.

Cherish me as I cherish you. Rejoice in my joy; sustain me through my pain.

When the day is bright, delight me with the warmth of your affection. When the night is dark, comfort me with the strength of your support.

Let us commit ourselves fully and freely to our shared happiness, however time may change us. Though the leaves on the trees may wither in winter, yet they revive in the spring.

May ours be a love for all seasons. May our union be blessed and last the lifetime that we now begin together.

Your group has three tasks:

a Consider the facts about marriage given on the previous page. Put forward your own explanations of them.

b Say, with reasons, which of the three forms of 'commitment' quoted you personally would choose if you were about to get married. You may, of course, decide that there are reasons for not choosing any of them – in which case, say what the reasons are.

c Discuss whether marriage will be, or ought to be, an outdated institution in the twenty-first century.

Now read *Telling Stories*

TELLING STORIES

People always said that Irene had total recall. She seemed to remember the smallest details of things they had long forgotten – the words of old pop songs, the shades of old lipsticks, minute-by-minute reconstructions of important events like Graduation Day, or people's weddings. If ever you wanted a step-by-step account of times past, they said to each other: ask Irene.

Irene rarely took herself through the evening before the day she was due to be married. But if she had to then she could have done it with no difficulty. It wasn't hard to remember the smells: the lilac in the garden, the polish on all the furniture, the orange blossom in the house. She even remembered the rich smell of the handcream that she was massaging carefully into her hands when she heard the door bell ring. It must be a late present, she thought, or possibly yet another fussy aunt who had come up from the country for the ceremony and arrived like a homing pigeon at the house.

She was surprised to hear Andrew's voice, talking to her younger sister downstairs. Andrew was meant to be at his home dealing with all his relations just as Irene had been doing. He had an uncle, a priest, flying in from the African Missions to assist at the wedding. Andrew's grandmother was a demanding old lady who regarded every gathering as in some way centring around her; Irene was surprised that Andrew had been allowed to escape.

Rosemary, her sister and one of the bridesmaids, had no interest in anything apart from the possible appearance of a huge spot on her face. She waved Andrew airily up the stairs.

'She's been up there titivating herself for hours,' Irene heard her say. Before she had time to react to Rosemary's tactlessness, Irene heard Andrew say 'Oh God,' in a funny, choked sort of voice, and before he even came into the room, she knew something was very wrong.

Andrew's face was as white as the dress that hung between sheets of tissue paper on the outside of the big mahogany wardrobe. His hands shook and trembled like the branches of the beautiful laburnum tree outside her window, the yellow blossom shaking in the summer breeze.

He tried to take her hand but she was covered in handcream. Irene decided that somehow it was imperative that she keep rubbing the cream still further in. It was like not walking on the crack in the road: if she kept massaging her hands then he couldn't take them in his, and he couldn't tell her what awful thing he was about to tell her.

On and on she went rhythmically, almost hypnotically, as if she were pulling on tight gloves. Her hands never stopped moving; her face never moved at all.

He fumbled for words, but Irene didn't help him.

The words came eventually, tumbling over each other, contradicting each other even, punctuated with apology and self-disgust. It wasn't that there was anyone else, Lord no, and it wasn't even as if he had stopped loving her, in many ways he had never loved her more than now, looking at her and knowing that he was destroying all their dreams and their hopes, but he had thought about it very seriously, and the truth was that he wasn't ready, he wasn't old enough, maybe technically he was old enough, but in his heart he didn't feel old enough to settle down, he wasn't certain enough that this was the Right Thing. For either of them, he added hastily, wanting Irene to know that it was in her interests as well as his.

On and on, she worked the cream into her hands and wrists; even a little way up her arms.

She sat impassively on her little blue bedroom-stool, her frilly dressing-table behind her. There were no tears, no tantrums. There were not even any words. Eventually he could speak no more.

'Oh Irene, say something for God's sake, tell me how much you hate me, what I've done to your life.' He almost begged to be railed against.

She spoke slowly, her voice was very calm. 'But of course I don't hate you,' she said, as if explaining something to a slow-witted child. 'I love you, I always will, and let's look at what you've done to my life...You've changed it certainly...' Her eyes fell on the wedding dress.

Andrew started again. Guilt and shame poured from him in a torrent released by her unexpected gentleness. He would take it upon himself to explain to everyone, he would tell her parents now. He would explain everything to the guests, he would see that the presents were returned. He would try to compensate her family financially for all the expense they had gone to. If everyone thought this was the right thing to do he would go abroad, to a faraway place like Australia or Canada or Africa...somewhere they needed young lawyers, a place where nobody from here need ever look at him again and remember all the trouble he had caused.

And then suddenly he realised that he and he alone was doing the talking; Irene sat still, apart from those curious hand movements, as if she had not heard or understood what he was saying. A look of horror came over his face; perhaps she did not understand.

'I mean it, Irene,' he said simply. 'I really do mean it, you know, I wish I didn't.'

'I know you mean it.' Her voice was steady, her eyes were clear. She did understand.

Andrew clutched at a straw. 'Perhaps *you* feel the same. Perhaps we *both* want to get out of it? Is that what you are saying?' He was so eager to believe it, his face almost shone with enthusiasm.

But there was no quarter here. In a voice that didn't shake, with no hint of a tear in her eye, Irene said that she loved him and would always love him. But that it was far better, if he felt he couldn't go through with it, that this should be discovered the night before the marriage, rather than the night after. This way at least one of them would be free to make a different marriage when the time came.

'Well both of us, surely?' Andrew was bewildered.

Irene shook her head. 'I can't see myself marrying anyone else but you,' she said. There was no blame, regret, accusation. Just a statement.

In the big house, where three hundred guests were expected tomorrow, it was curiously silent. Perhaps the breeze had died down; they couldn't even hear the flapping of the edges of the marquee on the lawn.

The silence was too long between them. But Andrew knew she was not going to break it. 'So what will we do? First, I mean?' he asked her.

She looked at him pleasantly as if he had asked what record he should put on the player. She said nothing.

'Tell our parents, I suppose, yours first. Are they downstairs?' he suggested.

'No, they're over at the golf club, they're having a little reception drink or something for those who aren't coming tomorrow.'

'Oh God,' Andrew said.

There was another silence.

'Do you think we should go and tell *my* parents then? Grandmother will need some time to get adjusted...'

Irene considered this. 'Possibly,' she said. But it was unsatisfactory.

'Or maybe the caterers,' Andrew said. 'I saw them bustling around setting things up...' His voice broke. He seemed about to cry. 'Oh God, Irene, it's a terrible mess.'

'I know,' she agreed, as if they were talking about a rain cloud or some other unavoidable irritation to the day.

'And I suppose I should tell Martin, he's been fussing so much about the etiquette of it all and getting things in the right order. In a way he may be relieved...' Andrew gave a nervous little laugh but hastily corrected himself. 'But sorry, of course, mainly sorry, of course, very, very sorry that things haven't worked out.'

'Yes. Of course,' Irene agreed politely.

'And the bridesmaids? Don't you think we should tell Rosemary now, and Catherine? And that you should ring Rita and tell her...and tell her...that... well that...'

'Tell her what, exactly?'

'Well, tell her that we've changed our minds...'

'That you've changed your mind, to be strictly honest,' Irene said.

'Yes, but you agree,' he pleaded.

'What do I agree?'

'That if it is the Wrong Thing to do, then it were better we know now than tomorrow when it's all too late and we are man and wife till death...' his voice ran out.

'Ah yes, but you don't see, I don't think we *are* doing the Wrong Thing getting married.'

'But you agreed...' He was in a panic.

'Oh, of course I agreed, Andrew, I mean what on earth would be the point of not agreeing? Naturally we can't go through with it. But that's not to say that *I'm* calling it off.'

'No, no, but does that matter as much as telling people...I mean now that we know that it won't take place, isn't it unfair to people to let them think that it will?'

'Yes and no.'

'But we can't have them making the food, getting dressed...'

'I know.' She was thoughtful.

'I want to do what's best, what's most fair,' Andrew said. And he did, Irene could see that, in the situation which he had brought about, he still wanted to be fair.

'Let's see,' she suggested. 'Who is going to be most hurt by all this?'

He thought about it. 'Your parents probably, they've gone to all this trouble...' He waved towards the garden where three hundred merrymakers had planned to stroll.

'No, I don't think they're the most hurt.'

'Well, maybe my uncle, the whole way back from Africa and he had to ask permission from a bishop. Or my grandmother...or the bridesmaids. They won't get a chance to dress up.' Andrew struggled to be fair.

'I think that I am the one who will be most hurt.' Irene's voice wasn't even slightly raised. It was as if she had given the problem equally dispassionate judgement.

'I mean, my parents have other daughters. There'll be Rosemary and Catherine, one day they'll have weddings. And your uncle, the priest...well he'll have a bit of a holiday. No, I think I am the one who is *most* upset, I'm not going to marry the man I love, have the life I thought I was going to.'

'I know, I know.' He sounded like someone sympathising over a bereavement.

'So I thought that perhaps you'd let me handle it *my* way.'

'Of course, Irene, that's why I'm here, whatever you say.'

'I say we shouldn't tell anyone anything. Not tonight.'

'I won't change my mind, in case that's what you're thinking.'

'Lord no, why should you? It's much too serious to be flitting about, chopping and changing.'

He handed their future into her hands. 'Do it whatever way you want. Just let me know and I'll do it.' He was prepared to pay any price to get the wedding called off.

But Irene didn't allow herself the time to think about that. 'Let me be the one not to turn up,' she said. 'Let me be seen to be the partner who had second thoughts. That way at least I get out of it with some dignity.'

He agreed. Grooms had been left standing at the altar before. He would always say afterwards that he had been greatly hurt but he respected Irene's decision.

'And you won't tell *anyone*?' she made him promise.

'Maybe Martin?' he suggested.

'Particularly not Martin, he'd give the game away. In the church you must be seen to be waiting for me.'

'But your father and mother...is it fair to leave it to the last minute?'

'They'd prefer to think that I let you down rather than the other way. Who wants a daughter who has been abandoned by the groom?'

'It's not that...' he began.

'I *know* that, silly, but not everyone else does.' She had stopped creaming her hands. They talked like old friends and conspirators. The thing would only succeed if nobody had an inkling.

'And afterwards...' He seemed very eager to know every step of her plan.

'Afterwards...' Irene was thoughtful. 'Oh, afterwards we can go along being friends...until you meet someone else...People will admire you, think you are very forgiving, too tolerant even...there'll be no awkwardness. No embarrassment.'

Andrew stood at the gate of the big house to wave goodbye; she sat by her window under the great laburnum tree and waved back. She was a girl in a million. What a pity he hadn't met her later. Or proposed to her later, when he was *ready* to be married. Hs stomach lurched at the thought of the mayhem they were about to unleash the following day. He went home with a heavy heart to hear stories of the Missions from his uncle the priest, and tales of long-gone grandeur from his grandmother.

Martin had read many books on being best man. Possibly too many.

'It's only natural for you to be nervous,' he said to Andrew at least forty times. 'It's only natural for you to worry about your speech, but remember the most important thing is to thank Irene's parents for giving her to you.'

When they heard the loud sniffs from Andrew's grandmother, the best man had soothing remarks also. 'It's only natural for elderly females to cry at weddings,' he said.

Andrew stood there, his stomach like lead. Since marriage was instituted, no groom had stood like this in the certain knowledge that his bride was not just a little late, or held up in traffic, or adjusting her veil – all the excuses that Martin was busy hissing into his ear.

He felt a shame like he had never known, allowing all these three hundred people to assemble in a church for a ceremony that would not take place. He looked fearfully at the parish priest, and at his own uncle. It took some seconds for it to sink in that the congregation had risen to its feet, and that the organist had crashed into the familiar chords of 'Here Comes the Bride'.

He turned like any groom turns and saw Irene, perfectly at ease on her father's arm, smiling to the left and smiling to the right.

With his mouth wide open and his face whiter than the dress she wore, he looked into her eyes. He felt Martin's fingers in his ribs and he stepped forward to stand beside her.

Despite her famous recall, Irene never told that story to anyone. She only talked about it once to Andrew, on their honeymoon, when he tried to go over the events himself. And in all the years that followed, it had been *so* obvious that she had taken the right decision, run the right risk and realised that their marriage was the Right Thing, there was no point in talking about it at all.

MAEVE BINCHY

2 Post-reading activity on *Telling Stories*

Speaking and listening *Making mood graphs*

During the story, Andrew's and Irene's feelings change a great deal. Sometimes both characters are distressed and disturbed. At other points, they are calm and composed.

a **With a partner**, draw the outlines of two 'mood graphs' – one for Andrew and one for Irene – on a large sheet of graph paper. Do it like this:

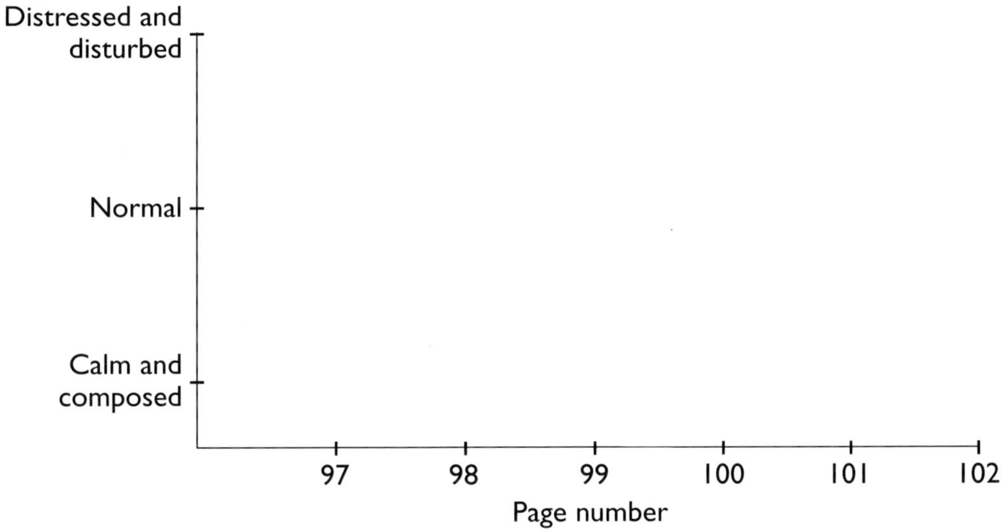

b Look back through the story and trace the 'ups and downs' of both characters' feelings. Fill in your graph as follows:

- Decide when Andrew feels at his *most* distressed and disturbed (i.e. at his least calm and composed). On your graph for him, make a small X to show on which page this occurs. Then do the same on Irene's graph.

- Next, decide when Andrew feels at his *least* distressed and disturbed (i.e. at his most calm and composed). On your graph for him, make a small X to show on which page this occurs. Then do the same on Irene's graph.

- Now take each page of the story in turn and plot the other ups and downs in the feelings of Andrew and Irene.

c Join up all your crosses on both graphs. This will give you a page-by-page diagram of each character's changes in mood throughout the story.

e **Join up with another pair** and compare graphs. If there are major differences, investigate why.

Comment on what the graphs show about:

- which character is more distressed and disturbed overall by the events described in the story.
- the relationship between the times when Irene feels most calm and composed and the times when Andrew does.

3 Text focus

Reading for understanding

a **In a group**, re-read what Andrew says to Irene about calling off their wedding. Then discuss the following questions:

- What are his reasons for wanting to cancel it?
- Do you feel they are selfish reasons?
- Do you think he is being completely sincere?

b Remind yourselves of Irene's reactions to the idea of not going ahead with the wedding. Then discuss the following questions:

- Does she agree with Andrew?
- Do you feel she is being more unselfish than selfish in the way she reacts to his change of mind?
- Do you think she does The Right Thing in the end?

c **As a class**, decide which of the two characters is the more mature in personality, attitude and behaviour. Do this by making 'maturity columns' for Andrew and Irene and filling them in with as many examples as you can find from the story.

d Finish your discussion by saying whether you think either, both, or neither of them is ready for marriage.

e **By yourself**, write character profiles of Andrew and Irene. On the basis of your view of each of them, say whether you feel that their marriage really *is* The Right Thing.

Reading and response

f **As a class**, or **in groups**, consider three aspects of Maeve Binchy's story-telling technique by discussing the questions which follow:

Conversational tone

How does the tone of voice in which the characters speak affect our view of them?

(i) **With a partner**, read aloud the following section of the story as if it were an extract from a play: From 'Oh God' (page 97) to 'No embarrassment' (page 101).

- Decide who will play Andrew and who will play Irene. Then read the whole section to yourself, slowly. Try to hear in your head the tone of voice both characters use as they speak.
- Then read the section aloud, missing out all of the writer's own descriptions. Speak only the characters' actual words.
- Now perform the extract, putting as much suitable expression into your voice as possible.

(ii) **As a class**, discuss what the tone of voice Andrew and Irene use reveals about their respective characters. Quote examples from the extract you have just read aloud to back up what you say.

Viewpoint

In the course of the story, the viewpoint changes from Irene's to Andrew's. Discuss exactly where this change takes place and how it does so. What do you think Maeve Binchy adds to her story by shifting the viewpoint in this way?

Flashback

(i) Re-read the first and last paragraphs of the story. How do you know that, apart from these two paragraphs, the whole narrative is written in the form of a flashback?

(ii) Does this device affect your response to *Telling Stories*? If so, give a full explanation of why it does so.

g **By yourself**, write an explanation of why Maeve Binchy chooses to tell so much of this story through dialogue. Quote from the text to support the points you make.

4 Written activities linked to *Telling Stories*

By yourself, write on one or more of the following topics:

a 'She [Irene] only talked about it once to Andrew, on their honeymoon, when he tried to go over the events himself.'

In dialogue form, write the conversation Irene and Andrew have about the unusual way they came to be married.

How will each of them look back on 'the events?' Now they are married, will they both see things in the same light, or will Andrew feel differently from Irene? How will they see their future together?

b Look back to Activity 1.

Imagine that you are about to be married. You have decided not to use the traditional marriage service but, together with your future husband/wife, to write your own form of words as a way of making your commitment to each other.

Explain what considerations would influence you. Then write your personal marriage vows.

c In your opinion, why do such a high proportion of marriages end in divorce or separation? What, if anything, could be done to remedy this situation?

Put forward your views in the form of a discussion essay. Argue your points fully, supporting them with evidence drawn from personal observation and/or research.

Now read *One Wednesday Afternoon*

ONE WEDNESDAY AFTERNOON

Excitement boiled in the woman and overflowed in an almost incoherent torrent of words in which the gatekeeper's puny inquiry bobbed for a second, unheeded, and was lost.

'An accident, y'say?' he asked again as the woman caught at her breath. 'Jack Lister?'

Her vigorous nod set heavy flesh trembling on cheeks and chin. 'His wife…I'm his mother. They've taken her to hospital.'

'Just a minute, then.' The gatekeeper went into the gate-house and the woman watched him through the dusty side-window as he lifted the receiver of the telephone and spoke to someone inside the low sprawl of factory buildings. In a few minutes he came out again. 'He'll be out in a minute,' he said. He eased the peak of his uniform cap, then clasped his hands behind his back and rocked backwards and forwards, almost imperceptibly, on toes and heels as he looked down at the woman.

She said, 'Thank you,' repeating the words absently a moment later. Then suddenly, as though a tap had been turned on inside her, the gush of words started again. The gatekeeper listened placidly until she touched on the nature of the accident, when his face screwed itself into a grimace.

'Ooh, that's nasty,' he said. 'That's nasty.'

At first when the foreman spoke to him the man did not appear to understand. 'Somebody wanting me?' he said, knitting his eyebrows in perplexity.

'Aye, up at the gate. There's been a bit o' trouble or summat. I should go up an' see what's doin', if I were you.'

The man wiped his hands with slow, puzzled thoroughness on a piece of wool waste, then brushed the dark forelock off his brow. He was near his middle forties, of medium height, and thin, with a dark, gaunt, high-cheekboned face. His short black hair with its forelock helped to give him a curiously old-fashioned appearance, as though, once out of the faded boiler-suit and dark workshirt, his choice of leisure garments would be a stiff wing collar, high-fronted jacket, and narrow trousers with piping down the seams.

'I reckon I'd better, then,' he said in his soft, troubled voice; and laying aside the piece of waste, he made as if to walk away.

'I should take me coat,' the foreman said, and the man stopped. 'An' look – gerrit cleared up, whatever it is, afore you bother comin' back.'

More baffled and puzzled than ever, he said, 'Oh aye, right, thanks.' He reached for his jacket and cap on the hook behind the machine and with troubled perplexity still creasing his forehead, strode away among the clamour of the shop, passing along the walk through the ordered chaos of machines and jungle-like growth of compressed-air pipes to the door at the far end.

His mother hurried to meet him as he came out of the building into the yard, pulling on his jacket as he walked.

'It's Sylvia, Jack,' she blurted. 'She's had an accident.'

He stopped and stared at her, seeming to be wrested from his troubled absorption by her words and the sight of her, hatless and with the flowered apron visible under the unbuttoned coat. He gripped her by the upper arm, the flesh soft and yielding under his fingers. 'What's she done?' he said. 'What's happened?'

'They came to tell me, Jack. They've taken her to the infirmary. It's her hair – she's had her hair fast in a machine.'

'Oh! God,' he said.

She ran clumsily alongside him as he started for the gate. 'All that hair, Jack...She wouldn't have it cut short an' sensible. An' I bet she never even wore it fastened up like other women. She never should ha' gone out to work again anyway, but she wanted too much brass for lipstick an' donnin' up in fancy clothes...Your wage wouldn't do for her. Any decent woman would ha' been content to stop at home an' look after her bairn...I told her it wasn't right, an' she knew you didn't like it...It's a judgement on her, that's what it is...a judgement.'

They were outside the gate now and still her voice went on and on, clamouring at the edge of his mind and driving him deeper into confusion. Until he turned on her suddenly. 'Shurrup! Shurrup! I can't hear meself think.' He stood at the pavement-edge and rubbed his hand across his face. 'God,' he said in a whisper. 'Oh! God.'

'What time did it happen?' he said. 'Will they let me see her, d'you think? Did they say how bad it was?'

'Just after dinner-time, it was,' his mother said. 'They couldn't have above got started again...It sounded bad to me.'

He set off down the road to the bus stop. 'I'll go straight away. I'll get there as soon as I can...Surely they'll let me see her.'

They had to wait five minutes for a bus. The mother stood by the signpost while her son paced restlessly about by the bill-hoarding behind, his stoutly nailed working boots rasping on the flagstones. When at last the bus came he stepped quickly past her and on to the platform, looking back in vague surprise as she followed him.

'Are you comin' an' all?'

'Course I am.'

They took seats on the lower deck. It was early-closing day in Cressley and the bus was almost empty. There was something that rattled with the vibration of motion and he tried with a part of his mind to locate it. Was it a window, or the back of a seat?

'What about bairn?' he said, as he remembered.

'I took him next door. I had to. He'll be all right. Mrs Wilson'll see to him while we get back.'

He nodded. 'Aye, she's not a bad sort.'

He became conscious as they drew near the town of his greasy overall and that he needed a wash and a shave. As his mother, unable to keep silent, broke into the quiet with her sporadic bursts of talk he fretted quietly about going to the hospital in such a state, And slowly then, after the initial shock, real consciousness of the accident began to fill his mind and he stiffened in his seat, coming rigidly upright beside his mother's stout form and staring straight ahead, the big adam's apple jerking convulsively in the slack skin of his neck as he tried to swallow with a throat gone dry with fear. Until, as they alighted from the bus, everything was lost in an overwhelming panic that his wife would die before he could reach her, and he started towards the hospital with long urgent strides, stopping occasionally to mutter with soft, frantic impatience as his mother climbed the hill breathlessly behind him.

Inside the hospital they had to wait again, but the house surgeon, when he came, was young and very gentle.

'Are you her husband?' The man nodded dumbly, cap in hand. 'And you're her mother?'

The woman said, 'No, her mother an' father are dead. I'm *his* mother. They live with me, y'see.'

The doctor nodded and the man blurted, 'How is she, Doctor?'

'It was a nasty accident,' the doctor said carefully. 'I'm afraid a good deal of her scalp has gone.'

'Will it disfigure her?' the woman asked, her eyes fixed on the doctor's face.

The doctor frowned. I shouldn't worry about that,' he said evasively. 'It's really amazing what can be done nowadays.'

The man brought his eyes up from the floor. 'I…I'd like to see her if…'

'Well perhaps for a minute, if she's out of the anaesthetic, but no longer.' He left them and returned with a young nurse. 'She's in Victoria Ward. The nurse will take you up.'

When the woman made as if to follow her son, the doctor restrained her. 'Just one now. He won't be long. You can sit down in the waiting-room.'

Going up in the lift he began to feel faint. He had always hated hospitals. He realised the foolishness of his dislike; hospitals were places of healing and mercy. But his aversion was to physical suffering in others and here he felt surrounded, overwhelmed by it. The characteristic smell of the building seemed to grow stronger the farther they were carried from the outside world, and his stomach seemed empty of everything except nausea. At the door of the ward he was handed over to the sister, who led him down the triple row of beds to the screened-off corner, where she said, 'Just a minute,' and left him exposed to the eyes of the occupants of the ward who, to his furtive glances, seemed every one to have an arm or a leg raised and secured in some agonisingly unnatural position.

The sister reappeared. 'She's awake. Now no noise or excitement. I'll come back when your time's up.'

He tiptoed, ponderous in his heavy boots, behind the screen. She was lying there, her lips pale and bloodless, her face a dead, pasty white against the crisp skull-cap of bandages and the pillow under her head. Her eyes flickered open. 'Jack.' He swallowed painfully. 'Aye, it's on'y me, Sylvia. It's on'y Jack.' He pulled forward a chair and sat down, fiddling uneasily with his cap for a time before letting it slip to the floor between his knees.

She watched him, her eyes dull and heavy-lidded. 'It's a mess, Jack, in't it?' she whispered then.

He groped for something to say. 'How did it happen?'

'I don't know really. It was so sudden. I was just reachin' over for somethin' an' all of a sudden me hair was fast round the spindle an' it was pullin' me in...' She closed her eyes and her body trembled under the sheets. 'It was awful...'

'It's about time they had t'Factory Inspector round that place,' he said in an angry whisper. 'I've heard some tales about 'em.' He looked at her. 'Does it pain you much?'

She moved her head feebly. 'Not now...It did at first, but they give me somethin' to stop it a bit.' The beginnings of a bitter little smile touched her lips. 'This is one up for you an' your mother, in't it? It's your turn to crow now.'

'No,' he said urgently. 'No, it's not like that.' He stopped, wringing his hands in helplessness. He wanted to say more but he did not know how. There was so much that he should say to make her understand. The fifteen years difference in their ages had never seemed so great. But words had never come easily to him and now he was bogged down again in inarticulateness: lost, with all the wordless misunderstanding of their marriage between him and her. He made a little movement of his arm. If only he could touch her...But the sheets were drawn right up to her throat and his hand with its dirt-ringed nails and grease ingrained in every line was like a sacrilege hovering above their spotlessness.

The sister returned silently. 'You'll have to go now.' He sighed in mingled relief and despair.

The girl in the bed opened her eyes again as he stood up and replaced the chair. He made a last desperate attempt. 'I'll come again, as soon as they'll let me,' he said. 'An look, don't worry yerself about it, lass. It'll be all right. It won't make no difference. No difference at all.'

'Look after Peter,' she said, and tried to smile. 'So long, Jack.'

There was horror in the sunlight outside, and in the normality of the traffic passing along the main road at the bottom of the hill, and in the people going about their business, not knowing or caring that she lay helpless in that great building with half her scalp torn away. A young girl rode by on a bicycle, her long hair blowing out behind her. A picture came to him then of his wife's beautiful red-gold hair entwined in the oil-blue steel of the spindle and he closed his eyes and clutched at the wall as his senses swooned and the world spun about him.

His mother took his arm. 'Come on, Jack. You'll be all right now you're out in t'fresh air.'

She said little going down the hill, but on the bus she started to talk again. 'She won't be the same agin, Jack. You could tell the doctor didn't like to say. But I knew...This'll cure her vanity. She'll not be wantin' to do much gallivantin' again...'

He only half-heard her, his attention held by a view across rooftops where a factory chimney poured out smoke, thick and dark against the sky, like a woman's hair...

'Now'll be your chance to put your foot down,' his mother was saying. 'You should ha' done it long since. Now'll be your chance to show her who's boss—'

He put his hands to his face beside her. 'No,' he broke in. 'No, now's me chance to show her...'

'Show her what?' his mother said. 'Show her what, Jack?'

He dropped his hands and clenched his big-knuckled fists on his knees. 'Nowt,' he said, and the ferocity and anguish in that one word made her gape. 'Nowt...you wouldn't understand.'

STAN BARSTOW

5 Post-reading activity on *One Wednesday Afternoon*

Speaking and listening *Hot-seating Jack's mother*

Put Mrs Lister (Jack's mother) in the 'hot seat'. By careful questioning, explore her attitude towards Jack and Sylvia's marriage.

a **In a group**, re-read everything Mrs Lister says in the story. Discuss what you learn about:

- her attitude towards Sylvia's accident.
- her view of Sylvia as a wife and mother.
- the way she treats Jack.
- how she sees the future of her son's marriage.

b One member of your group plays the part of Mrs Lister. The others question her about the things listed in **a** above – and anything else they consider relevant. She must answer in role. The hot-seat session should last for about ten minutes.

c Finish this activity by discussing **as a class** what the story shows about Mrs Lister's influence on Jack and Sylvia's marriage.

6 Text focus

Reading for understanding

a **With a partner**, find all the evidence you can that Sylvia sees Jack and his mother as enemies united against her. Why do you think she has come to think of them in this way?

b **With the same partner**, look closely at what we learn about Jack's feelings when he discovers that his wife is badly hurt. Quote from the text to indicate precisely what these feelings are.

c **As a class**, discuss the reasons why Jack and Sylvia's marriage has, up to now, failed – and whether you feel the story indicates that things are likely to change in the future.

d **By yourself**, write an account of the obstacles which Jack and Sylvia have had to face in their marriage. Give your view about whether, after Sylvia's accident, there is more or less chance of the marriage succeeding.

Reading and response

e **As a class**, or **in groups**, consider three aspects of Stan Barstow's story-telling technique by discussing the questions which follow:

Minor characters

As well as Jack, Sylvia and Mrs Lister, three other characters play an important part in the story: the gatekeeper, the foreman at the factory where Jack works and the hospital doctor.

Re-read what each of these minor characters says. How does Stan Barstow use them to direct our attitude towards Sylvia's accident and Jack and Sylvia's marriage?

Viewpoint

(i) The viewpoint in this story changes several times. Examine the way it shifts from Mrs Lister, then to Jack, then to Sylvia. Discuss Stan Barstow's purpose in alternating the viewpoint in this way – and in this order.

(ii) From whose point of view would you say the last part of the story is written, after Jack and his mother leave the hospital? Why is this important in the context of the story as a whole?

Setting

(i) Re-read Stan Barstow's descriptions of the following four settings:

- The inside of the factory (the sentence on page 107 beginning 'He reached for his jacket…').
- The interior of the bus (the paragraph on page 108 beginning 'They took seats on the lower deck.').
- The inside of the hospital (the paragraph on page 109 beginning 'Going up in the lift he began to feel faint.').
- Sylvia's hospital bed (the sentence on page 110 beginning 'But the sheets were drawn right up…').

(ii) The descriptions of these different settings are remarkably precise. Do they do more than help us 'see' the events being described? Would you say they contribute in any way to bringing out the central themes of Stan Barstow's story?

7 Written activities linked to both stories

By yourself, write on one or more of the following topics:

a Imagine that after Sylvia recovers, she and Jack decide to try and revive their marriage by making a number of changes to the way they live. One of these is to move out of Mrs Lister's house and set up on their own.

From their new address, Jack writes a letter to his mother explaining their reasons for taking this step. His mother replies.

Write these two letters, using your knowledge of the characters of Jack and Mrs Lister to make them as realistic as possible.

b One of the many reasons Mrs Lister disapproves of Sylvia is that, as the mother of a young son, she still goes out to work.

What are your own opinions on young mothers taking a job or continuing with a career? Express your views in the form of a story, a discussion essay, or a playscript.

c Imagine a situation where a marriage is failing or 'on the rocks'. Both husband and wife keep personal diaries, in which they express their feelings about each other and their relationship in general.

Write a number of extracts from each diary.

d A growing number of couples now choose to live together rather than get married. In the form of a discussion essay, or a speech for a debate, put forward:

(i) your opinion about why many people nowadays prefer to live together rather than enter into marriage.

(ii) your own view, with reasons, about whether they are right to do so.

8 End-of-Unit written assignments

Write on one or more of the following titles. Refer closely to the stories to back up your ideas and comments.

Subject-matter and themes

a Compare the characters of Andrew in *Telling Stories* and Jack in *One Wednesday Afternoon*. With whom do you feel more sympathy? Why?

b Neither story has a title which indicates what it is really going to be about. Consider each title in turn. How is it, in fact, linked with the story's subject-matter and themes? Say, with reasons, whether you feel the titles are well chosen.

Story-telling techniques

c In the course of both these stories, the viewpoint changes at least once. Write an account of how it does so, and give your own explanation of why the writers make use of this device.

d Each story hinges on the change in a character's feelings. Show how Maeve Binchy and Stan Barstow bring out the alteration in Andrew's and Jack's feelings respectively. How are the changes described linked to the two stories' themes?

General

e Which of these stories has made you think more seriously about marriage? What thoughts on the subject have the two stories provoked?

UNIT SIX

BARRIERS

The Princess Who Stood On Her Own Two Feet

Jeanne Desy

The Princess Who Stood On Her Own Two Feet is a traditional fable with a decidedly modern twist. Eager to find a lover, the Princess meets her knight in shining armour. But will he have more in common with one of the dragons he boasts of killing?

Father and Son

Bernard MacLaverty

Father and Son is set in modern-day Belfast. In this case, the barrier is between two family members. But what has caused it? The story gives no easy answers. We are asked to work them out for ourselves and come to our own conclusions.

1 Pre-reading activity on *The Princess Who Stood On Her Own Two Feet*

Speaking and listening *Absolutely fabulous!*

a **In a group**, read the material below.

Definition of fable

The literal meaning of 'fabulous' is 'fable-like'. The dictionary defines a fable as:

❛a story, not founded on fact, conveying a moral; often of a supernatural kind, esp. with animals as characters; myths, legendary tales❜

Ancient examples

Pool your memories of the Greek writer Aesop's fable of 'The Tortoise and the Hare'. What happens in it, exactly? What moral or 'message' is it meant to illustrate?

Recall any more fables you have read by Aesop and other ancient writers. Say in each case what moral you think is being conveyed.

Modern fables

The fable has remained a popular story-form. James Thurber, a twentieth-century American writer, produced 'Fables in our Time', from which the following story comes. Take turns to read it aloud.

The Shrike and the Chipmunks (a shrike is a vicious bird of prey with a strong hooked beak, also known as 'the butcher-bird')

Once upon a time there were two chipmunks, a male and a female. The male chipmunk thought that arranging nuts in artistic patterns was more fun than just piling them up to see how many you could pile up. The female was all for piling up as many as you could. She told her husband that if he gave up making designs with the nuts there would be room in their large cave for a great many more and he would soon become the wealthiest chipmunk in the woods. But he would not let her interfere with his designs, so she flew into a rage and left him.

'The shrike will get you,' she said, 'because you are helpless and cannot look after yourself'. To be sure, the female chipmunk had not been gone three nights before the male had to dress for a banquet and could not find his studs or shirt or suspenders. So he couldn't go to the banquet, but that was just as well because all the chipmunks who did go were attacked and killed by a weasel.

The next day the shrike began hanging around outside the chipmunk's cave, waiting to catch him. The shrike couldn't get in because the doorway was clogged up with soiled laundry and dirty dishes. 'He will come out for a walk after breakfast and I will get him then,' thought the shrike. But the chipmunk slept all day and did not get up and have breakfast until after dark. Then he came out for a breath of air before beginning work on a new design. The shrike swooped down to snatch the chipmunk, but could not see very well on account of the dark, so he batted his head against an alder branch and was killed.

A few days later the female chipmunk returned and saw the awful mess the house was in. She went to the bed and shook her husband. 'What would you do without me?' she demanded. 'Just go on living, I guess,' he said. 'You wouldn't last five days,' she told him. She swept the house and did the dishes and sent out the laundry, and then she made the chipmunk get up and wash and dress. 'You can't be healthy if you lie in bed all day and never get any exercise,' she told him. So she took him for a walk in the bright sunshine and they were both caught and killed by the shrike's brother, a shrike named Stoop.

MORAL: Early to rise and early to bed makes a man healthy and wealthy and dead.

b **In the same group**, invent (but do not write) your own modern fable which must contain at least five of the 'ingredients' listed below. What else it includes is up to your group to decide.

- a glamorous film-star
- a flight in a helicopter
- an enchanted forest
- a talking poodle
- a stretch-limousine
- a poison dart
- a visit to a tropical island
- a killer shark
- a National Lottery Ticket
- a bomb
- a member of the Royal Family
- a crocodile
- a detective
- a tragic death

Give the fable a title and a moral which is clearly linked to what happens in it. When told, your fable should last about as long as it took you to read aloud 'The Shrike and the Chipmunks'.

c **Join up with another group**. Tell your fable to them and listen to theirs.

Now read *The Princess Who Stood On Her Own Two Feet*

THE PRINCESS WHO STOOD ON HER OWN TWO FEET

A long time ago in a kingdom by the sea there lived a Princess tall and bright as a sunflower. Whatever the royal tutors taught her, she mastered with ease. She could tally the royal treasure on her gold and silver abacus, and charm even the Wizard with her enchantments. In short, she had every gift but love, for in all the kingdom there was no suitable match for her.

So she played the zither and designed great tapestries and trained her finches to eat from her hand, for she had a way with animals.

Yet she was bored and lonely, as princesses often are, being a breed apart. Seeing her situation, the Wizard came to see her one day, a strange and elegant creature trotting along at his heels. The Princess clapped her hands in delight, for she loved anything odd.

'What is it?' she cried. The Wizard grimaced.

'Who knows?' he said. 'It's supposed to be something enchanted. I got it through the mail.' The Royal Wizard looked a little shamefaced. It was not the first time he had been taken in by mail-order promises.

'It won't turn into anything else,' he explained. 'It just is what it is.'

'But what is it?'

'They call it a dog,' the Wizard said. 'An Afghan hound.'

Since in this kingdom dogs had never been seen, the Princess was quite delighted. When she brushed the silky, golden dog, she secretly thought it looked rather like her, with its thin aristocratic features and delicate nose. Actually, the Wizard had thought so too, but you can never be sure what a Princess will take as an insult. In any case, the Princess and the dog became constant companions. It followed her on her morning rides and slept at the foot of her bed every night. When she talked, it watched her so attentively that she often thought it understood.

Still, a dog is a dog and not a Prince, and the Princess longed to marry. Often she sat at her window in the high tower, her embroidery idle in her aristocratic hands, and gazed down the road, dreaming of a handsome prince in flashing armour.

One summer day word came that the Prince of a neighbouring kingdom wished to discuss an alliance. The royal maids confided that he was dashing and princely, and the Princess's heart leaped with joy. Eagerly she awaited the betrothal feast.

When the Prince entered the great banquet hall and cast his dark, romantic gaze upon her, the Princess nearly swooned in her chair. She sat shyly while everyone toasted the Prince and the golden Princess and peace forever between the two kingdoms. The dog watched quietly from its accustomed place at her feet.

After many leisurely courses, the great feast ended, and the troubadours began to play. The Prince and Princess listened to the lyrical songs honouring their love, and she let him hold her hand under the table – an act noted with triumphant approval by the King and Queen. The Princess was filled with happiness that such a man would love her.

At last the troubadours swung into a waltz, and it was time for the Prince and Princess to lead the dance. Her heart bursting with joy, the Princess rose to take his arm. But as she rose to her feet, a great shadow darkened the Prince's face, and he stared at her as if stricken.

'What is it?' she cried. But the Prince would not speak, and dashed from the hall.

For a long time the Princess studied her mirror that night, wondering what the Prince had seen.

'If you could talk,' she said to the dog , 'you could tell me, I know it,' for the animal's eyes were bright and intelligent. 'What did I do wrong?'

The dog, in fact, *could* talk; it's just that nobody had ever asked him anything before.

'You didn't do anything,' he said. It's your height.'

'My height?' The Princess was more astonished by what the dog said rather than the fact that he said it. As an amateur wizard, she had heard of talking animals.

'But I am a Princess!' she wailed. 'I'm supposed to be tall.' For in her kingdom, all the royal family was tall, and the Princess the tallest of all, and she had thought that was the way things were supposed to be.

The dog privately marvelled at her naiveté, and explained that in the world outside this kingdom, men liked to be taller than their wives.

'But why?' asked the Princess.

The dog struggled to explain. 'They think if they're not, they can't...train falcons as well. Or something.' Now that he thought for a moment, he didn't know either.

'It's my legs,' she muttered. 'When we were sitting down, everything was fine. It's these darn long legs.' The dog cocked his head. He thought she had nice legs, and he was in a position to know. The Princess strode to the bell pull and summoned the Wizard.

'Okay,' she said when he arrived. 'I know the truth.'

'Who told you?' the Wizard asked. Somebody was in for a bit of a stay in irons.

'The dog.' The Wizard sighed. In fact, he had *known* the creature was enchanted.

'It's my height,' she continued bitterly. The Wizard nodded. 'I want you to make me shorter,' she said. 'A foot shorter, at least. Now.'

Using all his persuasive powers, which were considerable, the Wizard explained to her that he could not possibly do that. 'Fatter,' he said 'yes. Thinner, yes. Turn you into a raven, maybe. But shorter, no. I cannot make you even an inch shorter, my dear.'

The Princess was inconsolable.

Seeing her sorrow, the King sent his emissary to the neighboring kingdom with some very attractive offers. Finally the neighboring King and Queen agreed to persuade the Prince to give the match another chance. The Queen spoke to him grandly of chivalry and honor, and the King spoke to him privately of certain gambling debts.

In due course he arrived at the castle, where the Princess had taken to her canopied bed. They had a lovely romantic talk, with him at her bedside holding her hand, and the nobility, of course, standing respectfully at the foot of the bed, as such things are done. In truth, he found the Princess quite lovely when she was sitting or lying down.

'Come on,' he said, 'let's get some fresh air. We'll go riding.'

He had in mind a certain dragon in these parts, against whom he might display his talents. And so the Prince strode and the Princess slouched to the stables.

On a horse, as in a chair, the Princess was no taller than he, so they cantered along happily. Seeing an attractive hedge ahead, the Prince urged his mount into a gallop and sailed the hedge proudly. He turned to see her appreciation, only to find the Princess doing the same, and holding her seat quite gracefully. Truthfully, he felt like leaving again.

'Didn't anyone ever tell you,' he said coldly, 'that ladies ride side-saddle?' Well, of course they had, but the Princess always thought that that was a silly, unbalanced position that took all the fun out of riding. Now she apologised prettily and swung her legs around.

At length the Prince hurdled another fence, even more dashingly then before, and turned to see the Princess attempting to do the same thing. But riding side-saddle, she did not have a sure seat, and tumbled to the ground.

'Girls shouldn't jump,' the Prince told the air, as he helped her up.

But on her feet, she was again a head taller then he. She saw the dim displeasure in his eyes. Then, with truly royal impulsiveness, she made a decision to sacrifice for love. She crumpled to the ground.

'My legs,' she said. 'I can't stand.' The Prince swelled with pride, picked her up, and carried her back to the castle.

There the Royal Physician, the Wizard, and even the Witch examined her legs, with the nobility in attendance.

She was given infusions and teas and herbs and packs, but nothing worked. She simply could not stand.

'When there is nothing wrong but foolishness,' the Witch muttered, 'you can't fix it.' And she left. She had no patience with lovesickness.

The Prince lingered on day after day, as a guest of the King, while the Princess grew well and happy, although she did not stand. Carried to the window seat, she would sit happily and watch him stride around the room, describing his chivalric exploits, and she would sigh with contentment. The loss of the use of her legs seemed a small price to pay for such a man. The dog observed her without comment.

Since she was often idle now, the Princess practised witty and amusing sayings. She meant only to please the Prince, but he turned on her after one particularly subtle and clever remark and said sharply, 'Haven't you ever heard that women should be seen and not heard?'

The Princess sank into thought. She didn't quite understand the saying, but she sensed that it was somehow like her tallness. For just as he preferred her sitting, not standing, he seemed more pleased when she listened, and more remote when she talked.

The next day when the Prince came to her chambers he found the royal entourage gathered around her bed.

'What's the matter?' he asked. They told him the Princess could not speak, not for herbs or infusions or magic spells. And the Prince sat by the bed and held her hand and spoke to her gently, and she was given a slate to write her desires. All went well for several days. But the Prince was not a great reader, so she put the slate aside, and made conversation with only her eyes and her smile. The Prince told her daily how lovely she was, and then he occupied himself with princely pastimes. Much of the time her only companion was the dog.

One morning the Prince came to see her before he went hunting. His eyes fixed with disgust on the dog, who lay comfortably over her feet.

'Really,' the Prince said, 'sometimes you surprise me.' He went to strike the dog from the bed, but the Princess stayed his hand. He looked at her in amazement.

That night the Princess lay sleepless in the moonlight, and at last, hearing the castle fall silent, and knowing that nobody would catch her talking, she whispered to the dog, 'I don't know what I would do without you.'

'You'd better get used to the idea,' said the dog. 'The Prince doesn't like me.'

'He will never take you away.' The Princess hugged the dog fiercely. The dog looked at her skeptically and gave a little doggy cough.

'He took everything else away,' he said.

'No,' she said. 'I did that. I made myself…someone he could love.'

'I love you, too,' the dog said.

'Of course you do.' She scratched his ears.

'And,' said the dog, 'I loved you *then*.' The Princess lay a long time thinking before she finally slept.

Then next morning the Prince strode in more handsome and dashing than ever, although, oddly enough, the Princess could have sworn he was getting shorter.

As he leaned down to kiss her, his smile disappeared. She frowned a question at him: What's the matter?

'You've still *got* that thing,' he said, pointing to the dog. The Princess grabbed her slate.

'He is all I have,' she wrote hastily. The lady-in-waiting read it to the Prince.

'You have *me*,' the Prince said, his chin high. 'I believe you love that smelly thing more than you love me.' He strode (he never walked any other way) to the door.

'I *was* going to talk to you about the wedding feast,' he said, as he left. 'But now, never mind!'

The Princess wept softly and copiously, and the dog licked a tear from her trembling hand.

'What does he *want*?' she asked the dog.

'Roast dog for the wedding feast, I'd imagine,' he said. The Princess cried out in horror.

'Oh, not literally,' the dog said. 'But it follows.' And he would say no more.

At last the Princess called the Wizard and wrote on her slate what the dog had said. The Wizard sighed. How awkward. Talking animals were always so frank. He hemmed and hawed until the Princess glared to remind him that wizards are paid by royalty to advise and interpret – not to sigh.

'All right,' he said at last. 'Things always come in threes. Everything.'

The Princess looked at him blankly.

'Wishes always come in threes,' the Wizard said. 'And sacrifices, too. So far, you've given up walking. You've given up speech. One more to go.'

'Why does he want me to give up the dog?' she wrote.

The Wizard looked sorrowfully at her from under his bushy brows.

'Because you love it,' he said.

'But that takes nothing from him!' she scribbled. The Wizard smiled, thinking that the same thing could be said of her height and her speech.

'If you could convince him of that, my dear,' he said, 'you would be more skilled in magic than I.'

When he was gone, the Princess reached for her cards and cast her own fortune, muttering to herself. The dog watched bright-eyed as the wands of growth were covered by the swords of discord. When the ace of swords fell, the Princess gasped. The dog put a delicate paw on the card.

'You poor dumb thing,' she said, for it is hard to think of a dog any other way, whether it talks or not. 'You don't understand. That is death on a horse. Death to my love.'

'His banner is the white rose,' said the dog, looking at the card intently. 'He is also rebirth.' They heard the Prince's striding step outside the door.

'Quick', the Princess said. 'Under the bed.' The dog's large brown eyes spoke volumes, but he flattened and slid under the bed. And the Prince's visit was surprisingly jolly.

After some time the Prince looked around with imitation surprise. 'Something's missing,' he said. 'I know. It's that creature of yours. You know, I think I was allergic to it. I feel much better now that it's gone.' He thumped his chest to show how clear it was. The Princess grabbed her slate, wrote furiously, and thrust it at the Royal Physician.

'"He loved me,"' the Royal Physician read aloud.

'Not as I love you,' the Prince said earnestly. The Princess gestured impatiently for the reading to continue.

'That's not all she wrote,' the Royal Physician said. 'It says, "The dog loved me *then*."'

When everyone was gone, the dog crept out to find the Princess installed at her window seat thinking furiously.

'If I am to keep you,' she said to him, 'we shall have to disenchant you with the spells book.' The dog smiled, or seemed to. She cast dice, she drew pentigrams, she crossed rowan twigs and chanted every incantation in the index. Nothing worked. The dog was still a dog, silken, elegant, and seeming to grin in the heat. Finally the Princess clapped shut the last book and sank back.

'Nothing works,' she said. 'I don't know what we shall do. Meanwhile, when you hear anyone coming, hide in the cupboard or beneath the bed.'

'You're putting off the inevitable,' the dog told her sadly.

'I'll think of something,' she said. But she couldn't

At last it was the eve of her wedding day. While the rest of the castle buzzed with excitement, the Princess sat mute in her despair.

'I can't give you up and I can't take you!' she wailed. And the dog saw that she was feeling grave pain.

'Sometimes,' the dog said, looking beyond her shoulder, 'sometimes one must give up everything for love.' The Princess's lip trembled and she looked away.

'What will I *do*?' she cried again. The dog did not answer. She turned toward him and then fell to her knees in shock, for the dog lay motionless on the floor. For hours she sat weeping at his side, holding his lifeless paw.

At last she went to her cupboard and took out her wedding dress, which was of the softest whitest velvet. She wrapped the dog in its folds and picked him up gently.

Through the halls of the castle the Princess walked, and the nobility and chambermaids and royal bishops stopped in their busy preparations to watch her, for the Princess had not walked now for many months. To their astonished faces she said, 'I am going to bury the one who really loved me.'

On the steps of the castle she met the Prince, who was just dismounting and calling out jovial hearty things to his companions. So surprised was he to see her walking that he lost his footing and tumbled to the ground. She paused briefly to look down at him, held the dog closer to her body, and walked on. The Prince got up and went after her.

'What's going on here?' he asked. 'What are you doing? Isn't that your wedding dress?' She turned so he could see the dog's head where it nestled in her left arm.

'I thought you got rid of that thing weeks ago,' the Prince said.

It was difficult for him to find an emotion suitable to this complex situation. He tried feeling hurt.

'What you call "this thing,"' the Princess said, 'died to spare me pain. And I intend to bury him with honour.' The Prince only half heard her, for he was struck by another realisation.

'You're talking!'

'Yes.' She smiled.

Looking down at him, she said, 'I'm talking. The better to tell you good-bye. So good-bye.' And off she went. She could stride too, when she wanted to.

'Well, my dear,' the Queen said that night, when the Princess appeared in the throne room. 'You've made a proper mess of things. We have alliances to think of. I'm sure you're aware of the very complex negotiations you have quite ruined. Your duty as a Princess…'

'It is not necessarily my duty to sacrifice everything,' the Princess interrupted. 'And I have other duties: a Princess says what she thinks. A Princess stands on her own two feet. A Princess stands tall. And she does not betray those who love her.' Her royal parents did not reply. But they seemed to ponder her words.

The Princess lay awake that night for many hours. She was tired from the day's exertions, for she let no other hand dig the dog's grave or fill it, but she could not sleep without the warm weight of the dog across her feet, and the sound of his gentle breathing. At last she put on her cloak and slippers and stole through the silent castle out to the gravesite. There she mused upon love, and what she had given for love, and what the dog had given.

'How foolish we are,' she said aloud. 'For a stupid Prince I let my wise companion die.'

At last the Princess dried her tears on her hem and stirred herself to examine the white rose she had planted on the dog's grave. She watered it again with her little silver watering can. It looked as though it would live.

As she slipped to the castle through the ornamental gardens, she heard a quiet jingling near the gate. On the bridge there was silhouetted a horseman. The delicate silver bridles of his horse sparkled in the moonlight. She could see by his crested shield that he must be nobility, perhaps a Prince. Well, there was many an empty room in the castle tonight, with the wedding feast cancelled and all the guests gone home. She approached the rider.

He was quite an attractive fellow, thin with silky golden hair. She smiled up at him, admiring his lean and elegant hand on the reins.

'Where have you come from?' she asked.

He looked puzzled. 'Truthfully,' he replied, 'I can't remember. I know I have travelled a long dark road, but that is all I know.' He gave an odd little cough.

The Princess looked past him, where the road was bright in the moonlight.

'I see,' she said slowly. 'And what is your banner?' For she could not quite decipher it waving above him. He moved it down. A white rose on a black background.

'Death,' she breathed.

'No, no,' he said, smiling. 'Rebirth. And for that, a death is sometimes necessary.' He dismounted and bent to kiss the Princess's hand. She breathed a tiny prayer as he straightened up, but it was not answered. Indeed, he was several inches shorter than she was. The Princess straightened her spine.

'It is a pleasure to look up to a proud and beautiful lady,' the young Prince said, and his large brown eyes spoke volumes. The Princess blushed.

'We're still holding hands,' she said foolishly. The elegant Prince smiled, and kept hold of her hand, and they went toward the castle.

In the shadows the Wizard watched them benignly until they were out of sight. Then he turned to the fluffy black cat at his feet.

'Well, Mirabelle,' he said. 'One never knows the ways of enchantments.' The cat left off from licking one shoulder for a moment and regarded him, but said nothing. Mirabelle never had been much of a conversationalist.

'Ah, well,' the Wizard said. 'I gather from all this – I shall make a note – that sometimes one must sacrifice for love.'

Mirabelle looked intently at the Wizard. 'On the other hand,' the cat said at last, 'sometimes one must *refuse* to sacrifice.'

'Worth saying,' said the Wizard approvingly. 'And true. True.'

And then, because he had a weakness for talking animals, he took Mirabelle home for an extra dish of cream.

JEANNE DESY

2 Post-reading activity on *The Princess Who Stood On Her Own Two Feet*

Speaking and listening *Male chauvinism*

a **In a group**, find all the evidence you can that the Prince's attitudes and behaviour are those of a male chauvinist and note the Princess's reactions to his sexist treatment of her.

Set out your findings in the form of a note chart, like this:

Examples of Prince's male chauvinism	Princess's reaction to it
He says, 'Haven't you ever heard that women should be seen and not heard?' (page 122)	She decides to please the Prince by not speaking.

Identify at least six examples. Each member of your group should note them down.

c Now put the Prince in the 'hot seat' and question him about his attitudes towards women. Use your note chart as a reference point.

One member of your group plays the part of the Prince. The others act as questioners. Your hot-seat session should take ten to fifteen minutes.

Concentrate on making the Prince explain and justify his way of treating the opposite sex.

d Finish this activity by holding a **class discussion** on the following topic:

'*The Princess Who Stood On Her Own Two Feet* describes a woman who is, at first, the victim of male oppression but who eventually triumphs over it.'

3 Text focus

Reading for understanding

a This fable contains not one but several 'morals' or messages. **With a partner**, consider the story as a whole and list every moral for which you can find evidence from the text.

Join up with another pair and compare lists. Explain, by referring to the details of the story, why you have identified particular morals. If the other pair has included any that you have not, listen carefully to their reasons. You can, of course, disagree with what they say.

b **In a group**, consider the importance to the whole story of the Princess's dog. Make a list of all the functions it fulfils in helping to convey the writer's main themes.

How far would you agree with readers who feel that the dog is, in fact, the most important 'character' in the story?

c **As a class**, discuss whether this fable, which was written in 1988, has any real relevance to life today.

In the course of your discussion, consider the targets of the writer's satire – that is, the things she feels to be wrong or foolish and which she therefore holds up to criticism.

d **By yourself**, write an essay on the following topic:

These two comments occur at the end of the story:

- 'I gather from all this – I shall make a note – that sometimes one must sacrifice for love.'
- 'On the other hand…sometimes one must *refuse* to sacrifice.'

Show how Jeanne Desy explores both these themes in *The Princess Who Stood On Her Own Two Feet*. Which of them do you think the story brings out more strongly?

Reading and response

d **As a class**, or **in groups,** consider three aspects of Jeanne Desy's story-telling technique by discussing the questions which follow:

Narrative climax

The climax (or 'high point') of a story need not come at the end, although it often does.

In *The Princess Who Stood On Her On Two Feet*, there are two points which might be said to represent the story's climax:

- The moment when the Princess's dog dies.
- The Princess's meeting with the young prince at the very end.

In your opinion, which of these two points is the true narrative climax? Why? In reaching your decision, you need to take into account the story as a whole and your view about its main themes.

Characterisation

The characters in this story are not given names. They are all presented as caricatures. In other words, we are not meant to think of them as 'real' individual people but as stereotypes who represent certain human qualities which are timeless.

Why do you think Jeanne Desy has chosen to present her characters in this way? Do you find it to be an effective means of character portrayal? In your opinion, would the story's themes have been conveyed more clearly in a realistic story rather than through a fable such as this?

Symbolism

Writers of fables frequently use symbolism.

(i) Discuss the following symbols in *The Princess Who Stood On Her Own Two Feet*. What do you take their meaning to be?

- The slate on which the Princess communicates with the Prince.
- The ace of swords which the Princess turns up when using cards to tell her own fortune.
- The wedding dress the Princess uses to wrap round her dog before she buries it.
- The white rose which the Princess plants on her dog's grave.
- The emblem on the young prince's banner: a white rose against a black background.

(ii) Are there other symbols you have noticed in the course of the story? If so, discuss their meaning and importance.

e **By yourself**, draw on the discussion you have had in **d** above to write your own account of the way in which this story is told. In the course of your writing, make clear what you have learned about the typical form and style of a fable.

4 Written activities linked to *The Princess Who Stood On Her Own Two Feet*

By yourself, write on one or more of the following topics:

a Imagine that after the Prince is jilted on the eve of his wedding day, he meets up with a friend who is as much of a male chauvinist as himself. The Prince recounts the story of his courtship of the Princess and gives his own version of their relationship.

Write the Prince's conversation with his friend as a sketch for TV or radio. Your main purpose is to bring out the sexist character of the Prince.

b We are said to be living in an non-sexist society where both genders have equal status and opportunity – yet many people, like the writer of the story, would deny that this is really the case. They claim that prejudice against women is, in many ways, as great as ever. On the other hand, some people complain that 'positive discrimination' in *favour* of women is on the increase.

What are your opinions on this subject? Write in one of the following ways:

- Put forward your views in the form of a discussion essay entitled 'All men are equal, but men are more equal than women'.
- Write a speech for a formal debate in which you propose either that 'Sexism is still alive and kicking women in the teeth' or that 'Sexism is dead – or, at least, dying'.
- Make up a playscript or story which features someone of either gender with pronounced sexist characteristics. It is worth bearing in mind that sexism can be at its strongest when it is subtle rather than blatant.

c Write a fable of your own which is relevant to today's society. Either decide on a subject yourself or write your fable to illustrate one of these morals:

- Many Hands Make A Mess Of It
- Who Dares Loses
- A Friend In Need Is To Be Avoided
- Love Makes The World Go Mad
- Never Say Die – Just Keep Quiet

5 Pre-reading activity on *Father and Son*

Speaking and listening *Barriers and breakdowns*

a **In a group**, discuss the reasons why barriers which are difficult to break down sometimes grow up between different people.

Begin your discussion by exploring the possible causes of conflict and disagreement between two generations in the same family. As you talk, everyone should make their own note chart, like this:

Parents' generation	**Our generation**
Want their children to succeed academically at all costs	Want more out of life than schoolwork and exam qualifications
Most interested in making money and 'keeping up with the Jones's'	Most interested in making friends and enjoying new relationships

Include at least five points on your chart.

b Now conduct a similar discussion about what gives rise to barriers between people from different class and/or cultural backgrounds.

As above, everyone should make their own chart.

c Finish this activity by contributing to a **class discussion** on why the groups you have been looking at can become divided by so many different barriers.

Are these barriers insurmountable – or can you see ways in which they might be broken down?

Now read *Father and Son*

FATHER AND SON

Because I do not sleep well I hear my father rising to go to work. I know that in a few minutes he will come in to look at me sleeping. He will want to check that I came home last night. He will stand in his bare feet, his shoes and socks in his hand, looking at me. I will sleep for him. Downstairs I hear the snap of the switch on the kettle. I hear him not eating anything, going about the kitchen with a stomach full of wind. He will come again to look at me before he goes out to his work. He will want a conversation. He climbs the stairs and stands breathing through his nose with an empty lunch box in the crook of his arm, looking at me.

This is my son who let me down. I love him so much it hurts but he won't talk to me. He tells me nothing. I hear him groan and see his eyes flicker open. When he sees me he turns away, a heave of bedclothes in his wake.

'Wake up, son. I'm away to my work. Where are you going today?'

'What's it to you?'

'If I know what you're doing I don't worry as much.'

'Shit.'

I do not sleep. My father does not sleep. The sound of ambulances criss-crosses the dark. I sleep with daylight. It is safe. At night I hear his bare feet click as he lifts them, walking the lino. The front door shudders as he leaves.

My son is breaking my heart. It is already broken. Is it my fault there is no woman in the house? Is it my fault a good woman should die? His face was never softer than when after I had shaved. A baby pressed to my shaved cheek. Now his chin is sandpaper. He is a man. When he was a boy I took him fishing. I taught him how to tie a blood-knot, how to cast a fly, how to strike so the fish would not escape. How to play a fish. The green bus to quiet days in Toome. Him pestering me with questions. If I leave him alone he will break my heart anyway. I must speak to him. Tonight at tea. If he is in.

'You should be in your bed. A man of your age. It's past one.'

'Let me make you some tea.'

The boy shrugs and sits down. He takes up the paper between him and his father.

'What do you be doing out to this time?'

'Not again.'

'Answer me.'

'Talking.'
'Who with?'
'Friends. Just go to bed, Da, will you?'
'What do you talk about?'
'Nothing much.'
'Talk to me, son.'
'What about?'

My son, he looks confused. I want you to talk to me the way I hear you talk to people at the door. I want to hear you laugh with me like you used to. I want to know what you think. I want to know why you do not eat more. No more than pickings for four weeks. Your face is thin. Your fingers, orange with nicotine. I pulled you away from death once and now you will not talk to me. I want to know if you are in danger again.

'About...'
'You haven't shaved yet.'
'I'm just going to. The water in the kettle is hot.'
'Why do you shave at night?'
'Because in the morning my hand shakes.'

Your hand shakes in the morning, Da, because you're a coward. You think the world is waiting round the corner to blow your head off. A breakfast of two Valium and the rest of them rattling in your pocket, walking down the street to your work. Won't answer the door without looking out the bedroom window first. He's scared of his own shadow.

Son, you are living on borrowed time. Your hand shook when you got home. I have given you the life you now have. I fed you soup from a spoon when your own hand would have spilled it. Let me put my arm around your shoulders and let me listen to what is making you thin. At the weekend I will talk to him.

It is hard to tell if his bed has been slept in. It is always rumpled. I have not seen my son for two days. Then, on the radio, I hear he is dead. They give out his description. I drink milk. I cry.

But he comes in for his tea.

'Why don't you tell me where you are?'

'Because I never know where I am.'

My mother is dead but I have another one in her place. He is an old woman. He has been crying. I know he prays for me all the time. He used to dig the garden, grow vegetables and flowers for half the street. He used to fish. To take me fishing. Now he just waits. He sits and waits for me and the weeds have taken over. I would like to slap his face and make a man out of him.

'I let you go once – and look what happened.'

'Not this again.'

The boy curls his lip as if snagged on a fish-hook.

For two years I never heard a scrape from you. I read of London in the papers. Watched scenes from London on the news, looking over the reporter's shoulder at people walking in the street.

I know you, son, you are easily led. Then a doctor phoned for me at work. The poshest man I ever spoke to.

'I had to go and collect you. Like a dog.'

The boy had taken up a paper. He turns the pages noisily, crackling like fire.

'A new rig-out from Littlewoods.'

Socks, drawers, shirt, the lot. In a carrier bag. The doctor said he had to burn what was on you. I made you have your girl's hair cut. It was Belfast before we spoke. You had the taint of England in your voice.

'Today I thought you were dead.'

Every day you think I am dead. You live in fear. Of your own death. Peeping behind curtains, the radio always loud enough to drown any noise that might frighten you, double locking doors. When you think I am not looking you hold your stomach. You undress in the dark for fear of your shadow falling on the window-blind. At night you lie with the pillow over your head. By your bed a hatchet which you pretend to have forgotten to tidy away. Mice have more courage.

'Well I'm not dead.'

'Why don't you tell me where you go?'

'Look, Da, I have not touched the stuff since I came back. Right?'

'Why don't you have a girl like everybody else?'

'Oh fuck.'

He bundles the paper and hurls it in the corner and stamps up the stairs to his room. The old man shouts at the closed door.

'Go and wash your mouth out.'

He cries again, staring at the ceiling so that the tears run down to his ears.

My son, he is full of hatred. For me, for everything. He spits when he speaks. When he shouts his voice breaks high and he is like a woman. He grinds his teeth and his skin goes white about his mouth. His hands shake. All because I ask him where he goes. Perhaps I need to show him more love. Care for him more than I do.

I mount the stairs quietly to apologise. My son, I am sorry. I do it because I love you. Let me put my arm around you and talk like we used to on the bus from Toome. Why do you fight away from me?'

The door swings open and he pushes a hand-gun beneath the pillow. Seen long enough, black and squat, dull like a garden slug. He sits, my son, his hands idling empty, staring hatred.

'Why do you always spy on me, you nosey old bastard?' His voice breaks, his eyes bulge.

'What's that? Under your pillow?'

'It's none of your fucking business.'

He kicks the door closed in my face with his bare foot.

I am in the dark of the landing. I must pray for him. On my bended knees I will pray for him to be safe. Perhaps I did not see what I saw. Maybe I am mistaken. My son rides pillion on a motor-bike. Tonight I will not sleep. I do not think I will sleep again.

It is ten o'clock. The news begins. Like a woman I stand drying a plate, watching the headlines. There is a ring at the door. The boy answers it, his shirt-tail out. Voices in the hallway.

My son with friends. Talking. What he does not do with me.

There is a bang. A dish-cloth drops from my hand and I run to the kitchen door. Not believing, I look into the hallway. There is a strange smell. My son is lying on the floor, his head on the bottom stair, his feet on the threshold. The news has come to my door. The house is open to the night. There is no one else. I go to him with damp hands.

'Are you hurt?'

Blood is spilling from his nose.

They have punched you and you are not badly hurt. Your nose is bleeding. Something cold at the back of your neck.

I take my son's limp head in my hands and see a hole in his nose that should not be there. At the base of his nostril.

My son, let me put my arms around you.

BERNARD MACLAVERTY

6 Post-reading activity on *Father and Son*

Speaking and listening *Murder enquiry*

a **In a group**, imagine that you are the CID team responsible for investigating the son's death. His father, in a state of profound shock, is hospitalised and unable either to remember anything or to speak. The only information you have to work on is that contained in the story.

Your task is to build up a file on the son's lifestyle over the past two years, and on his possible involvement in crime, with drugs, and with terrorism in Northern Ireland.

Your investigation is made more difficult by the fact that, (i) for obvious reasons, you are unlikely to be helped by others involved in crime, especially if it is drugs-related; and, (ii) in Belfast, political terrorism is a sensitive issue about which members of the public are reluctant to speak out.

Nonetheless, this is a serious murder investigation. You need, therefore, to comb the story for clues and try to establish a picture of:

- the son's recent history, in Northern Ireland and in England.
- his typical way of life and his daily movements.
- his acquaintances.
- the most likely reasons for his murder.

...and anything else you feel to be relevant.

Share out the task in whatever way seems best to you. **As a group**, you must produce:

- a set of notes for the police report you will have to write.
- a plausible theory about why the son was killed.

b When you have taken your enquiry as far as possible, **join up with another group**. Compare your notes and your findings.

Has either group found evidence which the other has overlooked? Have the groups reached similar or different conclusions about why the son may have been murdered?

Discuss in detail what you have discovered from the evidence in the story.

7 Text focus

Reading for understanding

a **With a partner**, look through the whole story and decide:

- which sections are narrated by the father.
- which sections are narrated by the son.
- which sections are presented by the writer as short sections of dialogue between them.

b **In a group**, find examples of, and discuss the reasons for, the breakdown in communication between father and son. Make a note chart to record your findings, like this:

Father	**Son**
Feels his son has betrayed the upbringing he has been given – 'This is my son who let me down.' (page 132)	Feels contempt for his father's fearfulness – 'Your hand shakes in the morning, Da, because you're a coward.' (page 133)

Include at least six entries on your chart.

c **As a class**, discuss the whole picture Bernard MacLaverty creates of the relationship between father and son. Consider in particular:

- why the relationship is so strained.
- whether there is any closeness or affection left between the two.
- which character seems to suffer more from the barrier that has grown up between them.

d **By yourself**, write a detailed commentary on the son's attitudes towards his father and the father's feelings towards his son. What does the story reveal about the reasons for the state of their relationship? Refer closely to the text to support your comments.

Reading and response

e **As a class**, or **in groups**, consider three aspects of Bernard MacLaverty's story-telling technique by discussing the questions which follow:

Viewpoint

Father and Son is written from two viewpoints which alternate throughout the story. First we 'listen' to the father, then to the son. Occasionally there are short sections of dialogue presented without comment from the writer.

Why do you think Bernard MacLaverty has chosen to use this technique of two-person (or 'dual') narration, with the father and son speaking turn-by-turn in the first person? Does it help to bring out any of the story's themes that you have already explored?

Internal dialogue

The story is told by the father and son between them, but their dialogue is largely 'internal': that is, we hear more of their thoughts than the words they actually speak to one another.

(i) Look back to the first two paragraphs of the story. Try re-writing them in a more typical third-person narrative style. For example:

The father got out of bed, padded downstairs to the kitchen in his bare feet, and switched on the kettle. Upstairs, his son lay awake and heard him…

(ii) What are the main differences between these two ways of telling? Do you feel that Bernard MacLaverty gains anything by writing as if he is inside the minds of his characters?

How the story ends

(i) In the final section, the father says, 'The news has come to my door'. What does he mean?

(ii) Do you find the ending of *Father and Son* to be effective? How far do you feel that:

- it comes as a shock?
- it leaves us puzzled as to what exactly has happened?
- its sudden violence is not in keeping with the rest of the story?
- it is tacked on so that the writer can end his story on a sensational note?
- it fits in well with the main themes of the story as a whole?

f **By yourself**, draw on your discussion of **e** above to write an account of the unusual way in which *Father and Son* is told. Say whether or not you feel that Bernard MacLaverty's style of writing is suited to the story's themes, giving evidence from the text to back up your opinion.

8 Written activities linked to *Father and Son*

By yourself, write on one or more of the following topics:

a You are a reporter on a Belfast newspaper. Write the front-page story of the son's murder.

What you write will depend strongly on your own interpretation of Bernard MacLaverty's story. However you understand it, try to bring out in your newspaper report:

- the probable motive for the shooting.
- the way it was planned and carried out.
- the reactions of the father and the local community.

Use a suitable journalistic style, incorporating interviews with witnesses, comments from public figures, and any background information you feel is relevant. If you wish, produce your final version of the story on a computer.

b Using any form you consider appropriate, write about a parent–child relationship which is in the process of breaking down.

The age of the central characters is for you to decide: there is no necessity to make the 'child' a teenager. You may draw on personal experience for your writing, or make it entirely fictional.

c Write a story on a subject of your own choice in which, like Bernard MacLaverty, you use the technique of dual narration.

This technique can be used effectively to explore a variety of themes, not just the breakdown of communication between two people. The most important consideration is to have, before you start, a clear impression of your characters and the relationship between them.

d Since Bernard MacLaverty wrote *Father and Son*, there has been a reduction of terrorism in Northern Ireland and the beginnings of a political 'peace process', however unstable this might be.

In the form of a discussion essay or a speech for a debate, give your views on what is required for the peace process to continue and to become permanent.

9 End-of-Unit written assignments

Write on one or more of the following titles. Refer closely to the stories to back up your ideas and comments.

Subject-matter and themes

a Show how *The Princess Who Stood On Her Own Two Feet* and *Father and Son* are both concerned with relationships that fail. Compare the reasons why they do so, and say which of the two characters in each relationship arouses your sympathy more strongly.

b *The Princess Who Stood On Her Own Two Feet* explores the theme of sexism in today's society. *Father and Son* explores the theme of modern-day violence and crime. Which of these themes has interested you more as you have worked through this Unit? Explain why.

Story-telling techniques

c Both writers choose an original and unusual way of telling their stories. Jeanne Desy employs the fable form; Bernard MacLaverty uses the device of dual narration. Which technique have you found to be more effective in conveying the writers' themes? Refer to both stories in expressing your opinion.

d In neither story are the characters given names. Bearing in mind the different form and style in which Jeanne Desy and Bernard MacLaverty write, put forward your own explanation of why they have chosen to leave their characters nameless.

General

e *The Princess Who Stood On Her Own Two Feet* makes its point through humour, whereas *Father and Son* is a chilling, arguably tragic, story. Yet both writers deal with serious issues. Which of the two stories have you found to be more successful in making you think about the points they raise?

Unit notes

The following notes highlight the main narrative techniques to be found in each Unit.

UNIT 1: CRIMES

Plot and structure	• Devices for creating suspense. • Use of flashback.
Characterisation and viewpoint	• Character portrayal through dialogue. • Alternating viewpoint to direct readers' sympathies.
Style	• Internal monologue.

UNIT 2: FAMILIES

Plot and structure	• Development of conflict and dramatic tension. • Alternation of description and dialogue as a story-telling device.
Characterisation and viewpoint	• Character portrayal through relationships and character contrasts. • Use of viewpoint as a device for judging characters.
Style	• Juxtaposition of direct and indirect speech.
Setting	• Use of symbolic descriptions.

UNIT 3: HEARTACHES

Plot and structure	• Letter-writing format. • Episodic narrative structure. • Significance of beginnings and endings.
Characterisation and viewpoint	• First-person/third-person presentation. • Varied use of dialogue to convey an impression of character.
Style	• Uses and effects of humour. • Alternating past and present tenses to focus readers' response.

UNIT 4: MYSTERIES

Plot and structure	• Diary format. • Function of surprise endings.
Characterisation and viewpoint	• Inferential character presentation without authorial comment. • Partial/implicit viewpoint.
Setting	• Use of setting to evoke mystery. • Contrasting settings within a single story.
Style	• Text and sub-text.

UNIT 5: MARRIAGES

Plot and structure	• Retrospective narrative. • Plot development based on triangular relationship.
Characterisation and viewpoint	• Evocation of character through tone of voice and physical gesture. • The significance of minor characters. • Shifting viewpoints to deepen response to character.
Setting	• Semi-playscript style.
Style	• Precise description of settings to highlight key themes.

UNIT 6: BARRIERS

Plot and structure	• Use of fable and allegory. • Dual narration as a structural device.
Characterisation and viewpoint	• Use of caricature and stereotype to convey themes. • Character portrayal without authorial comment. • Third-person/first-person points of view. • Conflicting viewpoints within a single story.
Setting	• Use of symbolic settings.
Style	• Internal monologue.

Pre-twentieth-century stories for comparison

The stories listed below can be usefully compared with those included in this book and with each other.

Crimes

My Favourite Murder	Ambrose Bierce
The Beryl Coronet	Arthur Conan Doyle
Black Peter	Arthur Conan Doyle
The Ransom of Red Chief	O. Henry
A Bank Fraud	Rudyard Kipling
Our Spot	Guy de Maupassant
The Purloined Letter	Edgar Allan Poe
The Murders in the Rue Morgue	Edgar Allan Poe
The Professor's Yarn	Mark Twain
The Stolen White Elephant	Mark Twain

Families

A Marriageable Girl	Anton Chekov
Home	Anton Chekov
His New Mittens	Stephen Crane
The Son's Veto	Thomas Hardy
The Grave at the Handpost	Thomas Hardy
The Tree of Knowledge	Henry James
The Devil	Guy de Maupassant
Country Living	Guy de Maupassant
What Men Live By	Leo Tolstoy
Malachi's Cove	Anthony Trollope

Heartaches

Misfortune	Anton Chekov
Concerning Love	Anton Chekov
Her Letters	Kate Chopin
The Melancholy Hussar	Thomas Hardy
Enter a Dragoon	Thomas Hardy

The Outcasts of Poker Flat	Francis Bret Harte
Kidnapped	Rudyard Kipling
Rosalie Prudent	Guy de Maupassant
The Nightingale and the Rose	Oscar Wilde
The Birthday of the Infanta	Oscar Wilde

MYSTERIES

The Haunted House	Charles Dickens
The Signalman	Charles Dickens
The Withered Arm	Thomas Hardy
The Green Door	O. Henry
The Masque of the Red Death	Edgar Allan Poe
The Fall of the House of Usher	Edgar Allan Poe
The Queen of Spades	Alexander Pushkin
The Transferred Ghost	Frank Stanton
The £1,000,000 Bank Raid	Mark Twain
The Magic Shop	H. G. Wells

MARRIAGES

The Grasshopper	Anton Chekov
The Kiss	Kate Chopin
A Pair of Silk Stockings	Kate Chopin
The Bride Comes to Yellow Sky	Stephen Crane
Barbara of the House of Grebe	Thomas Hardy
To Please His Wife	Thomas Hardy
Georgie Porgie	Rudyard Kipling
In the Bedroom	Guy de Maupassant
The Conservatory	Guy de Maupassant

BARRIERS

Désirée's Baby	Kate Chopin
The Knife	Stephen Crane
A Mystery of Heroism	Stephen Crane
Beyond the Pale	Rudyard Kipling
The Story of Muhammad Din	Rudyard Kipling
In the Pride of his Youth	Rudyard Kipling
Vendetta	Guy de Maupassant
Mother Savage	Guy de Maupassant
How Much Land Does a Man Need?	Leo Tolstoy
A True Story	Mark Twain